THE CA
OF BEDDI

CW00919529

Ronald Michell

2. *The Tudor Hall at Beddington*

The Carews
of Beddington

Ronald Michell

London Borough of Sutton Libraries and Arts Services

ILLUSTRATIONS ACKNOWLEDGEMENTS

Nos.

[1] (Cover portrait) and 12: In the collection of the Duke of Buccleuch and Queensberry, K.T., Drumlanrig Castle, Dumfriesshire, Scotland.

4, 24: Photos: R. A. Michell.

6, 17: Reconstructions and drawings by R. A. Michell.

10: Photographic Survey and Record of Surrey, Croydon Public Library.

13: By gracious permission of Her Majesty the Queen.

15, 16, 19: Photos: The late Ivor G. Foster, ARIBA.

18, 20, 25, 35: National Portrait Gallery.

22: Greater London Council.

23, 31: Photos: George Jenkinson, by kind permission of the Rector of Beddington.

29: Photo: Judges Ltd., Hastings.

34: By kind permission of the Surrey Record Office, who hold the original.

38: Photo: French & Co., donated by Miss M. F. Kempsell.

Back Cover: Carew Arms by the late Mrs. J. M. Vincent.

Copies of these pictures are in Sutton Libraries' Local Collection; as are the other illustrations used.

DESIGN: SHIRLEY EDWARDS

First published 1981

London Borough of Sutton Libraries and Arts Services
Central Library, St. Nicholas Way, Sutton, Surrey
Tel: 01-661 5050

© Text: R. A. Michell

ISBN 0 907335 02 0

Printed by John Bentley (Printers) Ltd., Todmorden.
A member of the Dunn & Wilson Group Ltd.

Preface

It is twenty-seven years since I first moved to Wallington and twenty-six since I clambered through the mess of builder's litter in the place still known as The Royal Female Orphanage and saw between the ladders and scaffolding the mighty hammerbeams of Sir Richard Carew's great hall. It was a moment as thrilling as it was unexpected and in a sense I have been following the Carews ever since. I had the opportunity of working briefly with the new school and for six months devoured everything that I could find about the family who lived there. I was soon in difficulties. The standard histories of Surrey repeat the information that Nicholas Carreu, the first of the line, was Keeper of the Privy Seal to Edward III, but what did that mean? How did he achieve such eminence? Whom did he meet? And, above all, what was the village where he chose to settle really like in 1353?

The trained historian knows where the answers to such questions may be found but the ordinary reader does not. The trained historian also knows the limitations of our knowledge and prefaces his statements with such irritating qualifications as 'Probably' 'It is conjectured that–' or 'On balance it seems likely that–'. The bare skeleton of facts is often scanty enough and the attempt to clothe the fragments in the semblance of flesh borders upon the hopeless. But this book needs to be intelligible to the general reader and to make it so it has been necessary to write in the background making it a kind of social history in microcosm. The idea as it progressed pleased me, because though the documentation is mainly about a family who were wealthy, and often doubtless covetous and selfish, it is good to be reminded occasionally that their pride of family, riches, and luxury were possible through the labours of generations of humbler people whose lives flash only briefly into the limelight of history.

The book owes a great debt to the local history collection of Sutton libraries, the Beddington and Wallington part of which was begun originally by Mr. W. J. Hill. To Douglas Cluett and June Broughton of the present library staff, and to Miss Batchelor of Wallington library, my thanks are due for their unfailing courtesy and endless enthusiasm, and to the curator of Tenby museum, who enabled me to spend a pleasant day with Giraldus. I must also acknowledge a debt to Keith Pryer for conversations spread over many years and to Mrs. Joan Carew Richardson. Her help as a genealogist of distinction has been beyond measure and her patient and time-consuming combing of the records, particularly calendars of close and patent rolls has added a new dimension to this work. My son, Dr. A. R. Michell, has also passed on the results of his own researches; he discovered the document which is the basis of Chapter 5 and is reproduced here by courtesy of the Master and Fellows of Corpus Christi College, Cambridge. Due acknowledgement must also be made to one who can never read these lines, the Rev. H. G. Dodd, who in the early years of the century transcribed everything that he could find about his parish into a near unintelligible script, including the invaluable Carew Correspondence which he discovered amongst the Additional Manuscripts of the British Museum. Finally, thanks must go to the Borough Librarian of Sutton, Mr. Roy Smith, for the enlightened policy towards local studies which he has consistently pursued.

R. A. Michell
East Grinstead 1980

3. *Beddington in 1840 from a print by Thomas Allom*

CHAPTER ONE

Carews and Beddington

IN 1964, when the formation of the Greater London boroughs was under discussion, it was suggested that the as yet un-named 'Borough 21' should be called Sutton Carew. The proposal was out-voted in favour of the simpler, if less distinguished, name of Sutton. Had the discussion taken place four centuries earlier, there is little doubt that the name chosen would have been Beddington. The new borough was made up of five ancient settlements, all built along the line where springs bubble, and sometimes gush, out of the chalk downs to flow northwards towards the Thames. By Tudor times each village had some claim to historic importance. The long association of Cheam with the See of Canterbury was broken at the time of the Reformation, but the village acquired a reflected glory from its new neighbour, the Palace of Nonsuch. Sutton, one of the smaller of the villages, was an estate of Chertsey Abbey; Carshalton, largest and most picturesque, clustered around the spring-fed ponds whose waters, flowing into the river Wandle, turned the wheels of many mills. Next came Wallington, perhaps even smaller than Sutton, but, for reasons which are still unclear, giving its name to an administrative district that stretched from Mitcham to Chaldon in one direction and from Cheam to Addington in the other; but no King's Officer or Justice had met the folk moot on the village green for many centuries and the Hundred of Wallington had become little more than a territorial division. Wallington had no church; it was included with other declining hamlets at Bandon and Woodcote in the parish of Beddington, in the centre of which, alongside the Church of St. Mary the Virgin, was the large moated manor house with its deer park, gardens and water, that gave the place its importance.

This was the hub of a huge estate that began in Norbury, continued through Mitcham, included Carshalton, Wallington, Banstead, Walton on the Hill and Bletchingley, and, briefly, Sutton, Epsom, Coulsdon and Horley as well as farms in the parishes of Horne, Burstow and others in Sussex, Kent, and overseas in Calais. The family who were the proud possessors of such far-ranging lands had been established in Beddington for two centuries and were named Carew. It is a name that recurs throughout our history, and if few of those who bore it have reached the highest ranks, there was never a period when one or more Carews were not soldiers, courtiers, administrators, members of Parliament, lawyers, and land-owning gentry. There are few counties in the southern part of Britain which have not at some time known a branch that played a part in the history of local affairs. There were Carews in Pembroke, in Haccombe, in Mohuns Ottery, Stoke-Fleming, and Bickleigh. There are Carews in Ireland and in Cornwall. Carews held land in Berkshire, Suffolk, Hampshire, Dorset, Sussex and Kent as well as Surrey. There were, and may still be Carews of Lanteglos by Camelford, and the Carews of Antony who became Pole-Carews and Carew-Poles, and other collateral branches like the Carew-Gibsons. All these, and probably most lesser folk around the country who bear the name today are descended from one Walter Son of Other (as the Domesday book has it–we should probably call it Otto) a Saxon lord who served both Edward the Confessor and William I as Constable of Windsor Castle and Keeper of the Forest, with estates in Surrey, Hants, and Buckinghamshire and a capital mansion at Stanwell in Middlesex. Walter, whose wife was of Norman birth, sired four stalwart sons each of whom set about founding dynasties, using the surname of de Windsor, or FitzWalter at will.

The third son, Gerald, took to the seas with Arnulf de Montgomery and helped him to invade Pembrokeshire and to establish castles at various strong points. He was entrusted with the command of Pembroke Castle, 'a slender fortress of stakes and turf,' but on an impregnable limestone rock surrounded on three sides by water. In 1094 the south Welsh rose in revolt, the castles fell and the garrisons were slain until Pembroke alone remained intact. Despite desertions, and extremities of hunger, Gerald de Windsor held fast until the revolt had spent its force. His reward was command of the whole area and marriage to the glamorous young widow Nest who was the daughter of Rhys ap Tewdr, a prince of South Wales. As part of her dowry, the princess brought Gerald the castle and estate of Carew, six miles from Tenby.

Perhaps tough Marcher Barons should not marry out of their social class: the marriage, although it gave a name to the family, was a disaster. Nest bore her husband three sons and a daughter before falling hopelessly in love with her cousin Owain Cadwgan. Owain, presumably by arrangement, set fire to the castle in which Nest and her husband were sleeping and she, tearing up the floorboards, bundled Gerald to malodorous safety through the privy-shaft of their tower. She then allowed herself to be abducted by her lover. The pair wandered as exiles through Ireland until they were brought by the aggrieved Gerald before Henry I. The king was so impressed by the beauty of "Helen of Wales" that he pardoned them both, knighted Owain, and eventually took Nest to be his own mistress, leaving to Gerald the poor satisfaction of trapping Sir Owain with a body of his Flemish troops and murdering him.

The magnificent ruins of Carew Castle, standing at the head of one of the sea inlets of Milford Haven, could, until last year, be visited. It has now been declared to be unsafe, and unless funds can be found quickly, it will crumble away into an even worse state than the Parliamentarians left it during the Civil War.

The story of Gerald, Owain and the beautiful Nest, like so many legends, exists in several variants, and there is often a hard-headed modern historian able to prove that many of the romantic trimmings could not have taken place. Few could find fault with the contemporary statement that Nest had twelve children, *most of whom* were by Stephen of Cardigan, Gerald and Henry I, or deny that the Anglo-Norman-Welsh mixture was a good one. William, Gerald's eldest son, styled himself Lord 'of Carew' (or de Carrio, Carru, or Carreu, the spelling remained variable). Another son, David, entered the Church and became Bishop of St. David's Cathedral; the third, Maurice, joined the forces of Richard, Earl of Pembroke, commonly called Strongbow, in an expedition of conquest, into Ireland, and founded in that country yet another surviving dynasty, the Fitzgeralds. A daughter, named Angharad, was the mother of Gerald de Barri (usually called by his Latinized name Giraldus Cambrensis) one of the greatest of twelfth century scholars.

2

4. *Carew Castle, Pembrokshire*

Eight generations later, during which time the family interests had spread from the west country as far as Berkshire, a landless younger son named Nicholas settled in Beddington. This was in 1353; his descendants remained there until 1816.

Beddington lies almost exactly nine miles due south of Westminster. The name is practically unknown, except to those who live there. In 1937 it was swallowed whole by its one-time hamlet of Wallington and thirty-two years later Wallington itself was merged into the London Borough of Sutton. But it is a green place still, that has not yet shaken off its history. The best vantage point is the ridge where Queen Elizabeth I is said to have walked. Here, in a grove, depleted, but not denuded, now that the elms have gone, one can look towards the north and see only meadows, treetops and the grey tower of St. Mary's Church. In the foreground, traffic on the busy Croydon Road is out of sight, and almost out of sound, in the deep and ancient cutting through which it winds up towards the old village centre. The monstrous cooling towers of Croydon power station are hidden by the avenues of giant beeches and chestnuts that lead the eye across what was the Tudor deer-park. Beyond the park, Beddington Marsh stretches, as yet, free of bricks and mortar to the edges of Mitcham Common. The river Wandle makes its first appearance just outside Beddington and meanders through the park towards the lake that was once the mill-pond for Wallington Mill. Just beyond the church, looking red-brick and rather Victorian, which indeed it is on the outside, is the Manor House that replaces the one leased by young Nicholas Carew in 1353. If the description sounds idyllic, one has to confess that everything else is houses. Sixty years ago topographers waxed lyrical about the trees, ancient timber-frame buildings, and eighteenth century mansions that made up the village centre. All have now gone save for one much misused mansion. After the First World War the houses crumbled and their estates were sold off to the speculative builders. The fields are still giving place to the housing needs of London.

The documented history of Beddington begins about A.D. 900 when a very annoyed Bishop of Winchester grudgingly surrendered it to King Edward the Elder in a letter that contains the earliest village inventory.

> The land is now completely stocked, and when my lord first let it to me it was quite without stock and stripped bare by heathen men. [A reference to a Danish raid.] And I myself then acquired the stock for which it was afterwards available there . . . Now of the cattle which has survived this severe winter there are 9 full grown oxen and 114 full grown pigs and 50 wethers, besides the sheep and pigs which the herdsmen have the right to have, 20 of which are full grown; and there are 110 full grown sheep, and 7 bondsmen, and 20 flitches; and there was no more corn there than was prepared for the Bishop's farm [i.e. no surplus to send away] and there are 90 sown acres.

By the time of the Norman conquest the village was split between two Saxon lords named Ulf and Azor, a division which was continued by King William who granted Azor's lands to William de Wateville and those belonging to Ulf to Milo Crispin. The Domesday book records that each manor had two small watermills; there was a church, which lay in de Wateville's holding, and a population of about 215 villeins and cottagers as well as six slaves. Downstream, to the west, Wallington's thirty households, strung between the green and the river comprised a separate manor belonging to the king. To the west, Croydon was already a township centred around the summer palace of the Archbishops of Canterbury. One can guess that the limits of Domesday Beddington are marked by the church of St. Mary on one side and the remaining village mill on the other;

the hovels of the villeins were strung irregularly between, on the low hill overlooking the river, with perhaps a greater concentration of dwellings where the track we know as Beddington Lane crossed a broader, swifter flowing Wandle than now. South of the village, though not necessarily exactly on the present line, was Croydon Way along which the weary jurors trudged to make their Domesday depositions before the King's Officer awaiting them on Wallington Green. The track was well used, for the open-air Hundred Court met regularly, and everyone had to attend. South of Croydon Way, on ground that rose towards the downs, were the huge open fields where the villagers had their strip holdings; beyond, unfenced and uninhabited, the downland made rough pasture for their herds. The water-table was higher in Norman England than it is now, and it is probable that several streams trickled down through what are now dry valleys to join the river. To the north of the village the land was flat and infertile. It was partially water-logged and formed the village waste, a place where pigs and geese might forage, and one that provided timber, turf and brushwood. The meadows on either side of the river completed the village economy by providing the hay that kept the herds alive during the winter.

The land was valuable; with its mixed soils and plentiful waters it had been farmed intensively since long before the Romans came to these islands. Villages along the spring-line were rarely more than a mile apart and these, like Beddington, were usually subdivided into two or more manors, though each might be five miles long from forest in the north to open downs in the south. No building survives from this period. Houses of sticks and earth have, like the men who built them, turned to dust. Part of a broken font and a few carved stones are preserved in the church, though whether they were part of the Saxon church or Norman rebuild cannot now be said.

Changes of overlordship were frequent. If the holder fell under royal displeasure, or the direct line failed, the manor escheated to the king and was granted anew at the curious rent of a wooden crossbow worth twelve pence, payable every Pentecost. For the de Watevilles, and others who followed them, the lands in Beddington were only one of several manors that they owned, and no elaborate manor house was essential. An enclosure, a grange to store the produce, stables and a house resembling an aisled barn, perhaps alongside the church on the site of the present mansion, were the most that was required. It may well be that even this house did not exist at the earliest period, and the lord, during his periodic visits with his attendant men-at-arms may have moved into the house occupied by his steward. Manor Farm was to the east of Hilliers Lane, and the hill on which it stood would have been reasonably defensible by an alien lord and his French-speaking guards.

To the villeins the lord probably meant little, though some lords were more rapacious than others. He appeared with his retinue, ate up the produce of their labours, and, having hunted (through their fields if he so wished), in days or weeks rode away to another manor, or to court, or to military service; it made little difference to them. They appeared when summoned before his Manor court, paid fines for their misdemeanors and were tallaged to pay for the knighting of his sons or the marriage of his daughters. In addition to the peasants' agelong battle against the elements and the seasons, they suffered an extra hazard; on the very day that promised well they were liable to be called out by the reeve to labour in their lord's fields. They dug, they ploughed, and sowed the seed broadcast. The boys came out with their slings to keep the rooks out of the growing corn. They reaped and bound; whole families labouring together on their own lands and on their lord's. In years of plenty they collected pennies by selling surplus produce; in hard years the old and the weak starved. But they were not dumb slaves. Every manor had its customs, rarely written down, but known and remembered, and if the occasion arose, extended to their advantage. The peasants expected their lord to honour the customs as they themselves were bound to. If they often lost verbal battles they could at least argue. As the centuries passed, the lord ceased to be a remote, French-speaking conqueror, and the villages along the spring-line acquired their own resident families who at least spoke the same language as their tenants. One of the the earliest to do so was the slightly smaller of the two Beddington manors, which, from the time of King John, was the property of the Huscarles, a family whose name suggests that they had an English origin. The manor took the name from the family (or perhaps it was the other way round). A resident lord, even a part-time resident, for the Huscarles also owned estates in Berkshire, requires a manor house; and a village tradition, current in 1873, remembered that the Huscarles manor house stood by the north bank of the river near to the point where the lane crossed the ford.

In 1333 Sir Thomas Huscarle appointed Master William de Carreu to be chaplain of the free portion of Beddington Parish. The Beddington portion has been a matter of controversy ever since the early years of the fourteenth century, and none of the inquiries held since that time has ever been able to establish how or why it began. Sibyl de Wateville, a sister of the Domesday Book holder, presented the advowson of St. Mary's Church, in 1159, to the newly-formed Bermondsey Priory. The advowson included not only the right to appoint a rector to the church, but also a claim on the tithes payable by all the tenants for its support. For some reason, possibly because of a dispute with the holder of the second manor, the tithes on two hundred acres of land belonging to that manor, with a house and garden between the church and Croydon Lane, were set aside to maintain a second priest in the parish. Just what duties, if any, were involved is not known. It has been suggested* that the holder was a King's Clerk who received the appointment as a reward for royal service.

Master William de Carreu was no simple parish priest. He was the third son of Sir Nicholas, Baron Carreu of Moulsford, whose mail-clad effigy lies in the chancel of the church at Carew Cheriton. Sir Nicholas rebuilt much of the castle from which his ancestor had made his unsavoury escape, and held also the lordship of Moulsford, south of Reading. He died in 1311 leaving four sons to continue the family name. Sir John, the eldest, died in 1324 and William, acting in concert with his elder brother, Thomas, made a bid to take over the Moulsford property. They were evicted by Lord Talbot, John's father-in-law, acting, doubtless, on behalf of the widow. The disagreement was settled in 1331 in a complicated medieval process by which the property was to be held in chief by Thomas, who enfeoffed his brother of the manor whilst allowing part to his sister-in-law and part to maintain his mother.

In the same year, William and Thomas took part in a raid on Manorbier Castle stealing goods and chattels worth £500. It was probably another family squabble, as Manorbier is only a few miles from Carew and was held by a de Barri relative, but a servant was killed in the attack and Lord Talbot opted to try the brothers. When they failed to present themselves before the justices they were declared outlaws. Two years

* By Keith Pryer in "The Beddington Portion"

later William received the Beddington appointment almost as far from the scene of his misdeeds as it was possible to get.

Master William was already an ordained priest. His name occurs on a list of Canons of St. David's Cathedral dated 21st May 1328 and he maintained an interest there though the Cathedral can hardly have benefited often by his presence; possibly Beddington did not either. As an ambitious cleric of the knightly class, he may well have sought employment in the king's household. He would have been well acquainted with Sir Thomas Huscarle through the Berkshire connection. The Huscarles held Purley Magna, near enough to Moulsford for them to be neighbours. In 1348 the Bishop of Winchester gave a licence for Sir Thomas to add a private chapel to his Beddington manor house, and in addition to other legal businesses transacted on behalf of his patron, Master William probably acted as chaplain there.

Also in 1348, William was associated with a younger relative, Nicholas Carreu, in a land transaction in Horley (Surrey) on behalf of Sir Thomas, Lucy his wife, and their son Thomas. The degree of relationship between the two Carreus has proved impossible to establish with any certainty. Two genealogies, both dating back to the time of the Beddington Carews are in print. One, which appears in Manning and Bray would make Nicholas the youngest son of Sir Nicholas, Baron Carreu, and therefore a brother of William, while the second, printed by Lysons, shows him to be the youngest son of Sir John Carew who died in 1362, and the grand-nephew of Master William. For reasons which are discussed in detail in the appendix, neither relationship is satisfactory, and I have come to the conclusion that a possible explanation is that Nicholas with his brother John were both sons of Master William, perhaps born in wedlock before he took to the religious (!) life. To have a priestly father, while no bar to high office at the time, may have been thought discreditable by later family historians who simply omitted a generation from the family tree.

For William and Nicholas Carreu, though born into the knightly class, there were no estates waiting to be inherited. The choice, common to generations of well-born younger sons, was between the Army and the Church. William chose the latter, and it is probable that Nicholas also took minor orders which, while not precluding marriage, would confer benefit of clergy. On 30th June 1347, King Edward III gave his assent to the late election, in the Cathedral Church of St. David, of Master William de Carreu, canon of the said church, to be Bishop of that place. The Carews had always taken an almost proprietorial interest in Britain's smallest cathedral. Richard de Carew was bishop from 1256 to 1280, and David Martin (an uncle of William) had occupied the see between 1296 and 1328. Master William had obviously lived down his wild adventures, though how, as an absentee canon, he had secured election we shall never know. His enthronement, however, never took place. It was always a delicate matter whether King or Pope presented to the vacant sees and in this case the Pope, perhaps unknown to the King, had already nominated Master John of Thoresby as bishop. The election of Master William was set aside; with what sense of frustration he returned to the service of Sir Thomas Huscarle we can easily guess.

The larger of the two Beddington manors, which had once belonged to William de Wateville was currently held by Sir Richard Willoughby, who, in 1344, had paid a fine of 100 shillings for entry into the manor without royal permission. It was followed by a formal deed of release by the previous owner which was sealed in the "Chancery at the house of the Carmelite fathers" in Westminster. Sir Thomas Huscarle and William de

Carreu were witnesses of the deed. Huscarles and Willoughbys were more than neighbours, for Sir Thomas was married to Lucy Willoughby, heiress to her father. The hope was, obviously, that the two estates would eventually be joined under their son Thomas.

The year 1348, when Nicholas Carreu is first recorded as working with Master William, is, perhaps the time when he first saw Beddington. If he was born before William was enrolled as a canon of St. David's, he was in his early twenties, and to him, and to his countrymen, the year seemed to presage the beginning of a new era. The English victories in France culminated in the capture of Calais and brought a flood of looted goods into the country. In the words of the Walsingham chronicler, "There was no woman of any standing who had not her share of the spoils of Calais, Caen and other places across the Channel, such as clothes, furs, pillows and household utensils, tablecloths and necklaces, gold and silver cups, linen cloths and sheets." But the ships bringing home the victorious warriors with their loot also carried the germs of the most terrible affliction that Europe has ever known, the bubonic plague, which contemporaries were to call the black death. It raged throughout the land in 1349; whole villages were depopulated, the fields untended and the mills idle for lack of corn. The plague was followed by a murrain which killed off the cattle; and a further epidemic, nearly as deadly as the first, in 1361. Between a quarter and a third of the population died, and plague remained endemic until the final outbreak in 1665.

Idle lands reverted to the lords who lacked the tenants to grant them to. It may have been these problems which caused Sir Richard Willoughby to relinquish his estate; it was also a suitable moment for an ambitious man with capital to take advantage of the depression. On the 6th May 1352, William and Nicholas Carreu paid 5 marks to the king for a licence to take over the manor of Beddington at an annual rent of 20 marks. The grant was for their lifetime only, but the manor house was to be the home of their descendants for the next four hundred years.

Though he now held a landed estate, William had not given up his clerical ambitions. Two years later he made a loan, (perhaps bribe would be a better term), of the enormous sum of 1,000 marks to the Prior of Arundel, in recognition of which he was to receive 40 marks a year until such time as he was promoted by the Bishop of Chichester, the Earl of Arundel, or the Prior himself, to a benefice within the counties of Surrey or Sussex. This document, dated in June 1354, is the last entry in the Close rolls concerning William de Carreu. He is buried in St. Mary's Church, Beddington, where his undated grave, now lost, was noted during the seventeenth century by Lancaster Herald.

CHAPTER TWO

Nicholas Carreu

I T NEEDS a very great effort of the imagination to visualize the landscape as it appeared on the eve of the Black Death when the Carreus first saw the village where they were to settle. It is probable that, during the three centuries that had passed since the Norman conquest, the population had doubled, causing the spring-line villages to throw out daughter settlements upon the previously empty downlands. From Wallington a hollow way, worn between the common fields, led to the new village of Woodcote; while a track, northwards from Beddington, led towards Bandon. Both villages were deserted long before accurate maps were drawn, and it is unlikely that their sites will ever be established with certainty. The present distribution of the name Woodcote suggests that the 'new lands' were not nucleated around church or mill, but dispersed in the form of adjoining farms as may still be seen in wealden districts.

Away from the villages the highways were broad. The Statute of Winchester ordered in 1285 that bushes, woods, hedges or dykes be cut back for a distance of 200 feet on either side "so that there be no place whereby a man may lurk to do hurt." Most dwellings were single-storey cottages with earth walls and thatched roofs comprising at most a 'hall' and 'bower' such as Chaucer describes:

Ful sooty was her bower, and eke her hall
In which she ate full many a slender meal

About the cottage was an enclosure

A yard she had, enclosed all about
With sticks, and a dry ditch without

Within the yard Chaucer's poor widow kept her three cows, a sheep called Malle, her three large sows, and her chickens. Her diet, he says, consisted of

Milk and brown bread, in which she found no lack,
Singed bacon, and sometimes an egg or two

But if this represents Chaucer's idea of subsistence level, there were many in our four villages who were much above it. It is a fortunate chance that has preserved the parchment roll containing the names of all those villagers who paid tax in the year 1332. In that year, parliament granted Edward III a subsidy, or what we might term a wealth tax, based on the value of his subjects' movable goods. Townsmen paid at the rate of a tenth of the total value, and countrymen at a fifteenth. All but the very poor whose goods were worth less than five shillings had to pay. In Beddington village fifteen households were taxable; their names make an interesting roll-call at a time when surnames were only beginning to be used by ordinary folk. The lowest rate was eightpence, or two groats, more than a week's pay for a peasant worker, if he could get it. This was paid by Henry

5. St. Mary's Church, Beddington

the Smith, Stephen of Storton, John Gargat, Richard Rayson, Nicholas at Hill and John Croucher. Robert the Chapman was a little better off—he paid tenpence, and Richard at Gate and John at Pole, twelve. The next group were, by comparison, wealthy: Walter Sharp paid two shillings; John Lemman three shillings; and Thomas Corbet, whom we know from other sources to have been the King's Valet, paid three shillings and two pence for his goods in the manor house of Beddington Home where he lived. The Master of St. Thomas' Hospital was taxed two shillings and sixpence for a house and mill known as Frere's Manor in what is now Beddington Park. Sir Thomas Huscarle, owner of the other manor, paid six shillings and eightpence, while the wealthiest man in the village was one Simon Rote, of whom nothing else is known except that some of those named above, and others in Bandon, paid rent to him for their lands.*

In Wallington, twelve householders paid a total of twenty-four shillings and fourpence. They were headed by William Kyng, perhaps the steward of the manor, who paid five shillings and elevenpence. Woodcote paid thirty shillings contributed by the heads of fifteen households which included Roger and Walter Ate Green. The most curious name to occur in a Surrey village was Ferando de Spaigne who paid five shillings and elevenpence and was the wealthiest man in the settlement. But by far the largest village was Bandon; its thirty-one households paid a total of fifty-seven shillings making it twice the size of Beddington. The lord of the manor, Roger le Forester, paid seven shillings and a penny in tax, more than either Corbet or Huscarle. In 1349 he obtained permission for an oratory to be attached to his house. Wherever the village of Bandon lay, it was a long walk to St. Mary's church.

The catastrophe of 1349 brought a train of social unrest. The years before the plague had seen something of a surplus of labour which made it easy for the younger sons of villeins to pay a small chevage to their lords for permission to live away from the manor. They might settle elsewhere, or make their way to London; or, if they were adventurous, enlist for service in the king's wars. Even those who stayed at home found that their lords often preferred a rent in cash that could be used to hire free labour instead of receiving reluctant services from unwilling tenants.

The empty homesteads and untilled land changed all that. A labour shortage made lords more insistent on feudal rights that had lapsed over the years, while the need for their labour gave villeins a new sense of their own value. The country land-owners found themselves caught between a surly peasantry, a fall in the rents that they received, and a government that asked for more and more in subsidies to pay for the war in France. Their representatives in Parliament made complaint with a modern ring about 'the malice of servants who refuse to work without outrageous wages'. Parliament's response was to order the stocks for any who dared to ask for more in wages than had been payable in 1348. As they trudged to work in the fields, the peasants repeated the question that the hedge-priest John Ball was asking:

When Adam delved and Eve span
Who was then the gentleman?

Even the victory at Poitiers and the ultimate conclusion of a peace treaty was overshadowed by the return of the plague in 1361—'the mortality of children' they called it to distinguish it from the earlier outbreak. It was followed by a winter of unusual severity.

* It would be meaningless to translate the above values into new pence.

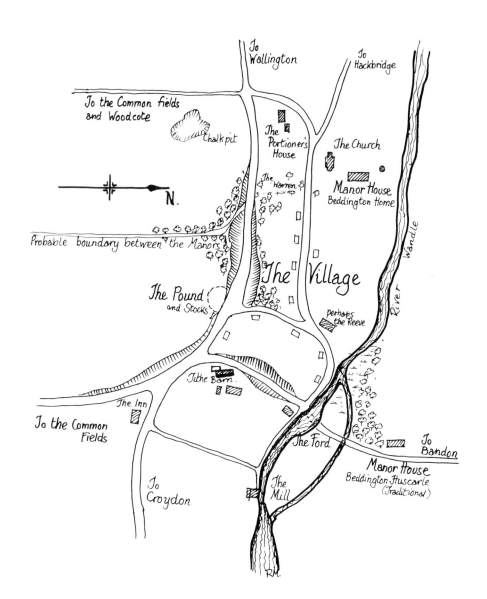

To Wallington

To Hackbridge

To the Common fields and Woodcote

Chalkpit

The Portioner's House

The Church

The Warren

Manor House
Beddington Home

N.

Probable boundary between the Manors

River Wandle

The Village

The Pound
and Stocks

perhaps
the Reeve

Tithe Barn

The Inn

To the Common Fields

The Ford

To Bandon

Manor House
Beddington Huscarle
(Traditional)

To Croydon

The Mill

R.M.

6. *Conjectural reconstruction of medieval Beddington*

In 1362 Nicholas Carreu served in Parliament as 'knight of the Shire' for the County of Surrey', but he did not sit again. During the next ten years he was obviously a valued servant of the king. Hardly a year passed without his name appearing on the Patent Rolls as being required to carry out some employment. He was sent as a justice with powers of 'oyer et terminer'* to many counties; he headed commissions of inquiry into 'wards, reliefs, escheats, and profits pertaining to the king'; he was appointed Commissioner of Array for the forces in Surrey, and became inspector of fisheries along the Thames. When one considers the difficulties of travel in medieval times it was a full life indeed. Perhaps he occasionally thought enviously of William of Wykeham who had entered the royal service at much the same time, received a handful of benefices made vacant by the plague, and was then ordained priest. In 1364 he became Keeper of the Privy Seal; two years later Bishop of Winchester; and, in 1368, as Chancellor, became the most powerful man in the kingdom.

The kings of England had always looked to the Church to provide men of education and ability who could fill the great offices of state; but, even in this, the time was ripe for change. It was understandable that there should be little love lost between able, hardworking and ambitious clerics and the great landowning magnates who could boast only of their acres and their noble lineage, but in the melting pot of social change the aristocrats were able to find allies amongst those commoners who blamed the privations they were suffering upon a greedy and negligent church. There were men like Carreu who were sufficiently well educated to perform a variety of duties required by the state, and there were many, both high and low, who were willing to listen to Wycliffe's teachings about the evils of a divided Papacy, political bishops, wealthy abbots, and absentee priests.

In 1369 the war with France broke out again, but it quickly degenerated into a series of squalid adventures that brought little glory, and no profit, to English arms. A series of defeats left only Calais, Bordeaux and Bayonne in English hands. An English fleet was defeated off La Rochelle, and there were fears of a French invasion in places as far apart as Sussex and Pembrokeshire. Edward III, the hero of Crécy, was lapsing into senility in the arms of his mistress, Alice Perrers, while the Black Prince, his body wracked with Spanish fever and his reputation sullied by massacres of civilians at Limoges, was carried home on a stretcher to await death in his palace of Kennington.

Leadership of the aristocratic party now passed to the king's third son, John of Gaunt, the Duke of Lancaster. To his supporters there was a simple reason for England's decline—the inept government of Wykham and the extortionate demands made by his church for funds which went to support a French Pope in Avignon. In the face of such powerful opposition William of Wykeham resigned his offices in 1372 and was replaced by dependable laymen belonging to the Duke's party. Sir Robert Thorpe became Chancellor, Lord Scrope Treasurer, and Nicholas Carreu Keeper of the Privy Seal. To this triumvirate was added Lord Latimer, Chamberlain and Keeper of the Privy Purse. Their task was to take control of the government at home while Lancaster led our forces to victory overseas. One wonders whether Carreu had any dealings with two other members of the Ducal party whose careers and achievement seemed so far beneath his own, Geoffrey Chaucer and John Wycliffe.

* 'To hear and to decide'

Wycliffe apart, there was very little altruism amongst the greater and lesser supporters of Lancaster. Each man around the ailing king held office for what he could get out of it. The greater the office the greater the rewards. Carreu must have worked very closely with Lord Latimer; both had offices in Westminster and seats on the Privy Council for which Nicholas acted as clerk. Latimer used a prominent City merchant, Richard Lyons, as the front man for his purchases, and Nicholas' name is also linked with that of Lyons as a joint holder of the manor of Delse near Rochester. His own dealings became manifold. He had already added considerably to his holdings of land. In 1359 the manor of Benchesham (a part of Norbury) was sold to him by Thomas de Gravesend, and two years later the latter issued a quitclaim giving up all rights in the manor. In 1369 Sir Thomas Huscarle died. Lucy Huscarle cannot have been young; her son Thomas had been of an age to associate with his father in land transactions in 1348, but Nicholas had known her for many years, and she was heiress to her father, Sir Richard Willoughby; moreover, if anything should happen to her son (and he seems to have died by 1371) she would also have some claim to the Huscarle estates.

No Carew could ever resist the attractions of a wealthy heiress. We do not know when Nicholas and Lucy were married, but in 1380 and 1381 Nicholas bought out the claims of the other heirs of Sir Thomas Huscarle, and, for the first time, perhaps, since Edward the Elder, Beddington was united under a single owner. Carshalton had also been split into a number of sub-manors, and, one by one, often like a modern developer working through intermediaries, Nicholas Carreu bought up their holdings. In the fourteenth century land was power, wealth, and status; industry was virtually non-existent, there were no banks, and movables might fall prey to the general lawlessness of the times. Land was security for heirs; marriage portions for daughters; and could buy masses for departed souls. The Carews pursued it whenever they might. Their strong boxes contained not coin, nor goods that moth could corrupt or thieves break in and steal, but parchment rolls of deeds, indentures, leases, tenures, jointures and life interests.

His position at court gave new opportunities. He purchased estates in Hertfordshire, and Berkshire. He became 'best friend' to the heir of his kinsman, Leonard Carew, which gave him the use of the family manor of Moulsford; he received from the king the manor of Willington in Bedfordshire during the minority of the young Earl of Nottingham; and a grant for life of the manor of Banstead which had been part of the establishment of the late Queen Philippa.

The change of leadership brought no joy to the English forces. John of Gaunt, with an army of 11,000 men, ravaged his way across France, without ever managing to fight a decisive engagement; lost his baggage train in floods at Auvergne; and arrived at Bordeaux in mid-winter with an army that had marched for the last six days without food.

In 1376 Parliament was again summoned to meet the continuing financial crisis. The Commons assembled in a disgruntled mood; their spokesman being Peter de la Mare, a Member for Herefordshire and seneschal to the Earl of March. Peter spoke out boldly about waste and corruption in high places, and, challenged by the Duke to name the offenders, named Richard Lyons, Lord Latimer and Alice Perrers. They were guilty, he denounced, of buying up all the merchandise that came into England and setting prices at their own pleasure whereby they made such a scarcity of things saleable that the common people could scarcely live. Such talk ensured that the Parliament of 1376 has passed into history as 'the Good Parliament'. Lyons and Latimer were summarily tried and imprisoned, Alice Perrers was sent packing, and a general redress of grievances was promised. The promises were never honoured; Alice Perrers returned to court; Latimer's impeachment was quashed; and it was Peter de la Mare who was sentenced to perpetual imprisonment in Nottingham Castle.

What was Nicholas Carreu doing during this period? He was not a member of the 'Good Parliament', nor of the 'Bad Parliament' which followed it and rapidly undid all its work. Between his court duties, he was apparently quietly attending to his own affairs, seeking out and buying up the claims of the various relatives of Sir Thomas Huscarle and consolidating his hold on his own estates. The Syndlesham family held some part of Huscarle's land, including the right to appoint the Portionist. These were renounced by William Syndlesham in 1363, and Nicholas installed his brother John in the living. (The rights had to be renegotiated with William's heir in 1372, and with his widow in 1381). Thomas Rote, son of the Simon who appeared in the subsidy list of 1323, surrendered his Beddington rents in 1376; and in the same year Nicholas obtained control of the Manor and other farms in the Isle of Grain from Thomas Malmaynes. The Carews subsequently quartered Malmaynes' arms with their own and it seems almost certain that Nicholas' first wife, otherwise unknown, was a daughter of this Thomas, in whose memory he installed two priests in a perpetual chantry in the little church of Stoke in the Isle of Grain.

Did Nicholas during these busy years change his allegiance? The conclusion that he owed his advancement to Lancaster's influence is inescapable. In 1372 the Duke had addressed a letter to him in terms of great friendship, "A nostre tres cher et bien ame Nicholas Carru". Even allowing for the fact that the purpose of the letter was to ask Carreu's help in obtaining a pardon for another protégé, the terms sound extremely cordial. Had there been a quarrel? Or was he just a quiet yes-man who sided with the dominant power of the moment? We cannot know.

On June 2nd 1377 the old king died; deserted, it was said, by his household. Even Alice Perrers left him, having first removed the rings from his stiffening fingers. The kingdom was in disorder; mobs attacked Lancaster's palace in the Strand; Wycliffe was under examination in St. Paul's for heresy, and when the Duke made an attempt to overawe the City he met such fierce resistance that he was forced to beat an ignominious retreat to the safety of Kennington. The heir to the throne was a boy of eleven. Was it time to change sides? Carreu's office ended with the old king's life, but as one of the executors of his will there remained much for him to do at the Court.

In the summer of 1380 he was named for a new task. The Earl of Pembroke had died in French captivity, and, the new Earl being a minor, Carreu, with others, was ordered to Haverfordwest as Justice of the Common Pleas. The west was strong in support of the Earl of March, and it may have been in Wales that he met Peter de la Mare, now released from jail and a popular hero. He may have been in the west during the following year when the long-threatened peasants' revolt took place. The Savoy Palace was gutted and burned by Wat Tyler's men, so was the Strand house of John Fordham, who had succeeded Nicholas as Keeper of the Privy Seal. His one-time business associate, Richard Lyons, was hacked to pieces by the infuriated mob.

At Christmas the Earl of March died in Cork, leaving an eight year old heir to the title. The young Earl became a royal ward and a group headed by Nicholas Carreu and Peter de la Mare shared out his estates. They included the town of Ludlow with its castle and other properties in Hereford, the March of Wales, and estates in Worcestershire,

Berkshire, and Essex.

Nicholas was an old man. For several years his eldest son, also named Nicholas, had been associated with him in the property deals which he had conducted on his own behalf. It was perhaps at this time that young Nicholas was married to Isabella De La Mare (she was probably the niece and not the daughter of Peter who is believed never to have married). On 13th October 1387 Nicholas wrote out his will in the manor house at Beddington. It is an indication of a major illness, for medieval people were superstitious about wills and tried to postpone the making of them until the last moment. The roll-call of his properties is staggering. He held the manors of Beddington, of Huscarle, of Carshalton and of Norbury outright, and had a life interest in the Royal manor of Banstead. In Beddington he listed a manor house, four watermills, 14 acres of meadow, and 100 acres of great wood; though perhaps with an eye to taxation, he noted that there was no underwood to sell and the pasture was covered with the branches of great trees. He also had 300 acres of arable and the same amount of pasture, a dove-house, and rents bringing in £4 per annum. Norbury had a manor house too, but this was a timber framed hall with perhaps a thatched roof which was regarded as of no value because of the amount of maintenance required; but the 100 acres of arable, 300 of pasture and 10 acres of meadow were of value, as were the rents received. In Woodmansterne he had acquired a third of the manor as well as farms called 'Chacombe' and 'Le Hoo'. In Nutfield, the manor and advowson of the church was his, as was a dwelling house with lands and woods in Chelsham. But these were only his Surrey properties. In Berkshire he retained the manor of Great Purley and a messuage at 'Tulleswyk', while in Kent he held the manors of Malmaynes on the Isle of Grain and Maytham near Rolvenden. It was no mean achievement for one born landless, who had survived the Black Death and the Peasants' revolt.

The illness of 1387 was not fatal, but thoughts of death remained with Nicholas. In 1389 he renewed the licence to found the chantry in memory of Thomas Malmaynes at the church of Stoke, as the previous attempt had been invalidated by a legal mistake. He died on 17th August 1390 having left explicit directions for his funeral. Thirteen poor men were to be clothed in black at his expense and were to hold thirteen torches at his burying. Five wax candles, each weighing six pounds, were to grace the altar of St. Mary's Church. Sums of money were to be given to various monastic houses so that masses might be said for his soul; while, in the church at Beddington, four suitable priests were to be appointed to pray for his own and all other Christian souls there. The misericordes which they used may still be seen in the chancel. He asked that his servants should be rewarded 'according to their deserts' and made bequests to two daughters, Lady Margaret Turbevyle and Lady Lucy, who was the Prioress of Rusper convent. There was also a small sum for his step-daughter, Johanna Huscarle, who was a nun. Finally, he bequeathed what was then a very large sum of £20 to rebuild St. Mary's Church.

CHAPTER THREE

Carews in service of their kings

NICHOLAS CARREU asked to be buried between his brother John and the church door; but no memorial marks the grave of the founder of the Beddington dynasty. The legacy of £20 was used for a complete rebuilding and probable enlargement of the church, and the graves of Nicholas and John may have been lost sight of; but the failure of the heir of so rich an inheritance to provide a worthy memorial to his father is difficult to explain.

Nicholas, the son, the new lord of Beddington, was at once appointed Sheriff of Surrey and Sussex for the year 1391. He served as knight of the shire in most of the Parliaments during the latter years of Richard II's reign, and in 1400, under Henry IV, he again became sheriff. All commentators have assumed, wrongly, that he was the son of Lucy Huscarle. At the time of his father's death the inquisition post mortem found him to be aged "28 and upward". This makes him seven years old when Sir Thomas Huscarle died and he must therefore have been the son of the unrecorded marriage to the heiress of Thomas Malmaynes. He was eighteen "and upward" when he associated with his father in the purchase of the Norbury estates, and seventy when he died in 1432, which makes sense of the reference to him at that time as an old man. It also makes the marriage of Nicholas Carreu and Lucy entirely one of convenience to link the two estates.

The sheriff (Scir gerefa or Shire reeve of Saxon times) was one of the oldest offices of government. During his year of office Nicholas was the representative of the king within the two counties. He was responsible for law and order and the administration of justice. He presided over the shire courts held twice yearly at Guildford and Lewes where he met representatives from the 'hundred' courts. He tried criminal cases in his own court, 'the Sheriff's Tourn', and supervised the election of the knights of the shire who were to represent the counties in parliament, with the right to annul the election if he thought the candidate unsuitable. He was captain of the 'Fyrd', or militia, and during his year of office received the king's justices when they arrived at the county towns, or at the halfway point in the still surviving 'Judges Row' at East Grinstead. They came to try the gravest cases, and also to inquire into his own stewardship of the king's interests. It was an office of great worship, but must have involved the holder in a very busy year.

His will shows that he had disposed of many of his outlying estates and had replaced them with a concentration of lands and farms in Surrey and Sussex. The principal manors of Beddington, Carshalton, Norbury and Nutfield remained the core of his holding. Banstead was gone; a few days after the death of the first Nicholas, Richard II had granted it to his knight Sir Reginald Braybrook. The Berkshire properties had also been traded away. In Sussex Nicholas had purchased the manors of 'Daddisham, Goring and Gretham', while in Surrey he named lands in 'Merstham, Sutton, Streatham, Croydon, Sanderstead, Warlingham, Cullesdon (Coulsdon), Woodmersthorne, Chipstead, Horlee, Blackinglegh, Micham, Burstowe, Horne, and Kershalton'.

The bulk of his property he left to Nicholas, the son of Isabella his first wife. Nicholas was the second son, an elder brother Thomas having died two years before his father, leaving daughters named Mary (Mercy) and Joan. His grand-daughters were well endowed by the will; Mary, who was married to Richard Ford, received the lands in Woodmansterne and Chipstead, while Joan, wife of William Saunder, was to have the Sanderstead and Warlingham property. The parish church at Charlwood has a charming souvenir of this union. The screen to the present chancel is richly carved with the initials R.S. intertwined with vine leaves and the arms of Saunder and Carew. This unique piece of Surrey woodwork was erected in 1480 by Richard Saunder the son of William and Joan.

Apart from endless land transactions, almost everything else that is known of the second Nicholas Carreu comes from the monuments in St. Mary's church. He is buried in the Chancel with Isabella and the memorial brass records in Latin that he died on the 4th day of September 1432, "an old man and full of days"–"senex et plenus dierum". He is shown as clean shaven with hair cut short and wearing a fur edged tunic with a high collar and large balloon sleeves drawn in at the wrist where one can see the close-fitting sleeves of an undergarment. The full tunic is confined around the waist by a narrow belt. Isabella wears a horned headdress covered by a veil which also conceals her hair. She has a high waisted gown with a deep turned-down collar and a jewelled girdle worn just below the breasts. Like her husband she wears a gown with huge balloon sleeves edged with fur, and an undergown showing at the wrists. Nestling against her long skirts is a tiny pet dog with a collar of bells. She bore three children, a son Thomas who died in 1430, a daughter who married Thomas Lewkenor and died in 1410 (this was recorded on a brass now lost) and another daughter, Isabel who outlived her father by only two years. Isabella may have been no more than twenty when she died. If this sounds a sad tale of mortality in early fifteenth century England, there is worse to come. Nicholas married again, this time to Mercy Hayme, and a brass hidden beneath the choir stalls tells the sad story of this marriage. It shows Philippa, a little girl who died in 1414. She is portrayed wearing a gown similar to Isabella but with a high stand-up collar. Her head is bare and encircled by a jewelled filet; beneath her effigy are shown head and shoulder portraits of her thirteen brothers and sisters who did not survive infancy, each with their name pathetically engraved beneath: Guy, John, John, John, John, William, William, Eleanor, Lucy, Agnes, Agnes, Margaret and Anne. Elsewhere in the chancel is a small brass to Margaret Oliver, the nurse to this tragic brood; does she need commiseration or blame for such a catalogue of mortality? When Nicholas came to be laid to rest in the chancel only two of his seventeen children were still alive, Isabel, soon to follow him to the grave, and her brother Nicholas.

The third Nicholas Carew (we will now use the modern spelling, although there are variations for another century) married Margaret, the daughter of Sir Roger Fiennes, who bore him two sons, Nicholas and James, and three daughters. He was a member of parliament in 1439; and was three times sheriff of the county, in 1440, 1444, and 1448. The country was passing through a lawless and violent phase of assassination and expropriation that was to erupt finally into open warfare. He is thought to have been a follower of the Duke of Exeter and in 1446 was one of those who was pardoned for

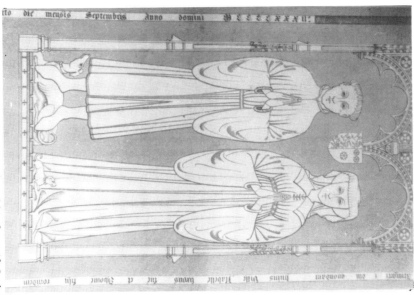

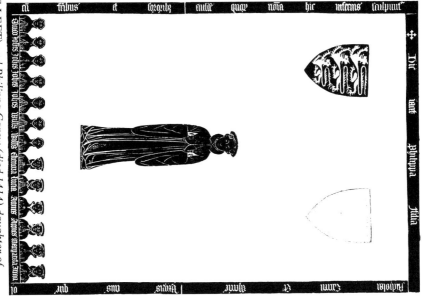

7, 8. *Nicholas Carew, (died 1432) and his first wife Isabella (ABOVE LEFT) and Philippa Carew (died 1414) daughter of Nicholas and his second wife Mercy Hayme; from brasses in St. Mary's Church Beddington*

having supported the wrong faction. He may have led a Surrey contingent to fight for the king at the first battle of St. Albans, because, in October 1455, he, with other prominent Lancastrians, was again pardoned. He died 20th April 1458 at the age of about fifty-three. One has a sense of a hardworking official who had little joy from his estates. He is buried at Beddington, but neither his widow to whom he left Beddington, Carshalton and Norbury for her lifetime, nor his two sons, nor his daughters, thought to provide him with a memorial tablet.

Young Nicholas (he was twenty-two when he inherited) had already followed the family tradition of service to the crown. He was King's Sergeant, and in 1457 was made Constable of Southampton at a salary of £10 a year.

In 1461, Edward, Duke of York, a grandson of that Earl of March whose estates the first Nicholas had managed, defeated the Lancastrians; and, after a dash to London, seized the crown and was proclaimed Edward IV. A few days later an order was issued from Westminster to Sir John Cobham and Nicholas Gaynsford, Sheriff, to arrest and imprison Nicholas Carew, the late Escheator of Surrey and Sussex and ten others. Gaynsford, who was later to prove an adept at changing sides, lived in neighbouring Carshalton in Stone Court. As a reward for his support, the new king also gave him the manor of Shalford. Perhaps he did not act quickly enough, or perhaps Nicholas was able to counter-petition Edward, for before the year was out, it was Gaynsford's turn to be in disgrace and a writ was despatched ordering the seizure of Carshalton and Shalford 'late belonging to the rebel and traitor, Nicholas Gaynsford'.

Both men seem to have been pardoned quickly, but the troubled times produced some very involved pieces of litigation. It appears that young Nicholas conspired with a 'joyner' and goldsmith from London, a tanner of Cobham, and twenty-two others to accuse a husbandman Richard Attewell of breaking into his house at Beddington and stealing four horses. Attewell was found to be innocent, but one of his accusers, named John Ware, was ordered to stand trial before the justices and subsequently outlawed when he failed to present himself for trial. Six years after the event, John Ware received a pardon claiming that he could not appear before the justices because he had already surrendered to the Marshalsea prison. The part played by Nicholas in this curious sequence cannot now be determined. More straightforward was the case which he conducted against his mother who had married again, to Walter Denys. In 1464 they were jointly sued by Nicholas Carew for damage done to the Norbury property which would one day come to him. He claimed that they had not only allowed the buildings to fall into disrepair, but his step-father had cut down and sold 600 oak trees worth six shillings and eightpence each, and 200 ash trees worth four shillings each. The law-suit, in itself unimportant, gives an idea of the afforestation in the northern parts of Croydon and also the information that Norbury manor house comprised a hall with chamber attached to it, a kitchen, bakehouse, cattleshed and stables, all under one roof.

His suit was apparently successful, but he died two years later on August 3rd 1466, aged only 30, leaving a widow (Margaret Langford), three young daughters, and a three-year-old son who made the fifth Nicholas in succession. It seems to have been understood that Norbury should be left for the suppport of the widow, because, much later, in 1494, the sisters tried unsuccessfully to get possession of Norbury on the strength of their mother's, or perhaps their grandmother's, inheritance. Meanwhile, Margaret was allowed to enjoy the profits of the estates on behalf of her son, but had to swear an oath that she would not marry without the consent of the king. The child was still alive in 1474

20

at which time his mother was married to John Carent of Ayssh, an ex-sheriff of Somerset. There had likely been another family upset because they were both pardoned their breach of the peace and trespasses. The date of death of the fifth Nicholas Carew is not known, but the estates were then taken over by the Crown and administered by Hugh Fenne and William Essex, both of them attorneys, pending an investigation as to who was the rightful heir. The court decided in favour of his uncle James, the second son of the third Nicholas. Being lawyers *and* royal representatives they were probably in no hurry to come to a decision and it seems possible (from a sentence in Manning and Bray) that they had not decided until after James was also dead.

James Carew is something of an enigma. He was named as one of the executors, but apparently not provided for, in his father's will. He set about finding his own estates, Carew-fashion, by marrying a double heiress named Eleanor who shared with her three sisters and a half-sister the lands of her father, Lord Hoo, and through her mother the lands of Lord Welles. Her half-sister married a wealthy London merchant, Sir Geoffrey Bulleyn and so became the ancestress of Henry VIII's ill-starred queen. About the time of her marriage, Eleanor's uncle, Lord Richard Welles, died violently. Caught up in the intrigues of the Wars of the Roses he was executed with Sir Thomas Dymock. In the four-way shareout of the lands, James Carew received only the manor of Wartling in Sussex, but it brought him a great deal of honour, as his descendants henceforward added the quarterings of Hoo and Welles to the three black lions on a golden shield which was the coat of arms shared with Carews everywhere. He may have done better out of the death of Dymock, who, in addition to holding lands in Lincolnshire, was lord of Wallington manor which was granted to the neighbouring Carew estates. It seems possible that while the lawyers prevaricated and Margaret his mother, Margaret his brother's widow, his three sisters and their respective husbands, fought to keep what they could of the estates, James lived out his life on the Sussex manor that came as his wife's inheritance, or perhaps at Great Maytham near Rolvenden where the church has a Carew portrait in glass of 1470. The only documents that have been traced concerning him are a list of rents due to him in Sussex, and, in 1490, a commission of array which lists him with other Sussex gentry. Wartling is about ten miles from Brede Place, the home of Sir Robert Oxenbridge, and it was at Brede that his son, Richard Carew, must have met the lady who was to become his wife.

Everything about James is a matter of speculation. Manning and Bray say explicitly that he was dead before the descent was settled, but the sentence is a little confused over all those Nicholas Carews. It has been suggested that he was the builder of the Carew chapel of St. Mary's Church, Beddington, but if he did so he has no tomb within it. On stylistic dating grounds it is thought that he may have been responsible for the great hall at Beddington, and as the man who stayed out of the limelight while the nobility destroyed itself he may well have been the builder of both. All that can be said for certain about him is that he ensured the survival of his family, and lived into more peaceful times. He died in 1492 during the reign of Henry VII.

His son, Richard, served in the hastily assembled royal army of 15,000 men who gathered at Blackheath on 17th June 1497. Here they confronted a crowd of 15,000 Cornishmen who had marched in a state of "greate agony and variaunce" to make a protest about taxation. Peaceful demonstrations were a thing unknown to the fifteenth century; many died in that not very glorious battle, including some 300 of the royal forces. Sir Richard Carew rode back to Beddington when it was all over, having been knighted on the field by the King's own hand.

Sir Richard Carew was appointed Sheriff of the county in 1501 for the now customary year of office, and was to serve the King in other capacities, notably as governor of Calais. He married Malyn, a daughter of Sir Robert Oxenbridge of Brede and widow of William Cheyney. He, I believe, rather than his father, is most likely to have been the builder of the Tudor great hall which remains one of the glories of Beddington.

The first Nicholas made out his will "at the Manor house at Beddyngton October 13th 1387" but, until recently, it has been very uncertain whether this building stood on the site near the church that was the home of later generations of his family. Until 1949 an extremely ancient building near the village centre known as "the old post office" was sometimes pointed out as the earliest home of the Carews, but the supposition was based solely upon its antiquity and its supposed status when it was built. At the time of its demolition it had been divided into four cottages, but it was easy to see that it had once been a single dwelling with central hall open to the roof trusses, and crosswings at either end. But we have seen that medieval Beddington boasted a number of families whose wealth approached that of the lords of the manor, and experts believe that the old post office could not have been built until thirty years after Nicholas Carreu sat down to make out his will. The fifteenth century saw a notable improvement in living standards, at least amongst the well-to-do, and may yeoman farmers built themselves hall-houses as large and impressive as the old post office. An examination of a recently acquired document in the Surrey Record Office now makes it reasonably certain that the earlier Carews lived in a moated dwelling alongside the church on the site now occupied by the present manor house.*

The central feature, as of all other medieval dwellings, of any status, was the hall, which need not have been large, and was probably timber framed with an open hearth in the centre of the earthern floor. The kitchen was a separate block connected with the hall through a passageway which led between the pantry, or dry store, and the buttery. The roughly contemporary little manor house at Cuddington for which a full survey was made for Henry VIII, had, in addition to this necessary living space, "thre parlers and chambers buylded square at the ends of the sayde hall with outcasts of bay windows above and below, . . . well glassed." The de Cuddingtons, whose status and connections never equalled that of the Carews, had, in addition, seven servants' chambers, and, at the kitchen end "two larder houses and in the same foure ovens", a large and a small barn, and a stable for six horses. The Carews can have had no less; their buildings were doubtless grouped around one or more courtyards, with a gate-house and drawbridge with which to cross the moat.

Moated manors were commoner in the weald than north of the downs, but the proximity of the Wandle River made it easy to provide, and the only other building in the district known to possess one was the Archbishop's Palace at Croydon. The moat lasted into the seventeenth century when draining and extensive repairs were made to it. Who constructed it is unknown, but if one had to made a guess, the first Nicholas Carreu is the most likely candidate.

Three major rebuildings, in c1500, 1710 and 1865, have removed all traces of the earliest manor house except perhaps for some of the stones in the cellars. The great hall and its associated cellars have survived the last two rebuildings and date from the Tudor

* See page 79

9. *The Old Post Office in the early years of the 20th century*

period. The hall shows the status to which the family aspired by the early fifteen hundreds. It is 60 feet 8 inches (18.5 m) long, 32 feet 4 inches (9.85 m) wide, and about 40 feet (12 m) high and is spanned by five great hammer-beam trusses with intricate tracery above the collar-beams and two tiers of wind-braces that link the trusses. In style it most resembles the Palace at Eltham, built for Edward IV, and in size it equals the Archbishop's hall at Croydon. Its precise dating is a matter for conjecture. Eltham Palace was built c1470 to 1480. D. J. Turner believes that the style and details of construction are sufficiently close to postulate that the same unknown master carpenter was responsible for both; Horace Walpole stated that the "fine old hall was copied by Wolsey at Hampton Court", which would make Sir Richard the builder—he almost certainly built the Carew Chapel of which he is the first occupant. Thomas Fuller, in 1670, named Sir Nicholas, Sir Richard's son; and Nicholas Pevsner, and others, ascribe it to Sir Francis, his grandson. Surrey Record Office has a document prepared by a steward named John Watts headed "Reparations there don a pon the manor by John Wattes by commandment of Sir Ric Carewe, Knight." The sixteen pages of accounts list expenses paid out for brickmaking as well as wages of carpenters and sawyers. If Watts was not building the great hall, he must have been doing a major work on everything else! Unfortunately there is no date, but John Watts is known to have accounted to Sir Richard in 1508, and this seems to be as near a date for the building of the hall as we are likely to arrive at.

One can glean a few more details about the house by the positioning of the cellars. A staircase led down from the buttery to the brick-vaulted wine cellar below. Racks for barrels may still be seen, as well as the chute by which they were delivered.* The Cuddington Manor also had "2 small Cellers whiche vsually served For the Pantry and botrye." There was a second cellar behind the hearth in the kitchen hall which was entered by a brick staircase alongside the chimney. The mark left by the stairs can be plainly seen, as can the base of the hearth with two small cupboard-like recesses that may once have served as proving ovens for bread. This semi-basement room was perhaps the pantry, but its principal purpose was to give access through a small four-centred doorway to a vaulted passage through which may have flowed a stream of fresh water from the moat. Other anomalous features can be seen in the existing cellars; what appears to be an earth sewer flowed beneath the kitchen and perhaps into the moat on the opposite side from the fresh water intake. However, investigations into these features are still in process and new discoveries may necessitate a revision of these conclusions. There are more cellars at the other end of the great hall where the parlours and bedchambers of the house were once to be found, but the later builders have left few clues as to how the rooms above were placed.

In 1509, when he embarked to take over his duties as Captain of the castle and garrison at Calais, Sir Richard left behind, in the care of John Watts, his wide-ranging acres graced by the finest manor house, Croydon excepted, in the whole of Surrey. His family had a satisfying record of royal service during the last century and a half, and Nicholas, his teenage son, was already established as a firm favourite of young Henry VIII. The future augured well.

---

* Dating of these features is uncertain, as they have been much altered.

10. *Tomb of Sir Richard Carew* (died 1520)

11. *Roof trusses in the Great Hall*

12. Portrait of Sir Nicholas Carew K.G. (executed in 1539) by Hans Holbein

CHAPTER FOUR

A King's Favourite

NICHOLAS CAREW was born about 1495 and for the rest of his life was never far from the court. Many years later he spoke of being "brought up under His Majesty since I was six years old", words that can only mean that he grew up in the Tudor palaces as a companion, or perhaps a page, to the prince who was one day to become Henry VIII. That the king was his boyhood hero is evident throughout his career, and the occasional overfamiliarities and estrangements speak of a close bond between them. Of course, Nicholas was not alone; a group of young men, all much the same age, became part of the intimate circle around Henry. There was one-eyed Francis Bryan, sailor and poet; Edward Neville and Harry Guildford, who, with Nicholas, were favourite riding and jousting companions; and John Peachey and Edward Poynts. All were eventually knighted and became gentlemen of the privy chamber; they drank and diced together, vied in all manner of athletic and martial feats, sang songs of love and bawdry far into the night, and pursued the court beauties. They were all of good county birth, and were grouped around the young heirs of the old nobility: Edward Stafford, Duke of Buckingham; Charles Brandon, who was created Duke of Suffolk; and Henry's first cousin, Henry Courtenay, Marquess of Exeter. They were the despair of the staid older generation of courtiers like Norfolk, Worcester and Wolsey.

The younger ladies of the court, maids of honour, wives and mistresses, joined in the fun, happy to catch the roving eye of their royal master. Bessy Blount, Jane Popyngcourt and later Mary Boleyn, in turn gave solace to Henry during the near continuous pregnancies of the queen. Francis Bryan's sister, Elizabeth, was introduced to the court circle, and she and Nicholas were married in 1514. She was a beauty, and may have been no more than fifteen when she came to court. She and Bessy Blount, another fifteen-year-old, were singled out for special greetings by Charles Brandon when he was on a mission to Paris.

It was a good match. Her father was vice-chamberlain to Queen Catherine of Aragon, and her mother became the official royal nurse, while Elizabeth was as high in the royal favour as was Nicholas himself. Sir Richard Carew settled the estates of Wallington, Beddington, Carshalton, Woodmansterne, Woodcote and Mitcham upon the newly married man. His own duties in Calais left him little time to enjoy them, but the lands can have meant very little to the young couple either, except as an income to be spent on their pleasures. In the words of the song that the king himself had written and composed:

> Pastance with good company
> I love and shall until I die

> Grudge who will, but none deny,
> So God be pleased this life will I
> For my pastime
> Hunt, sing, and dance,
> My heart is set,
> All goodly sport
> To my comfort
> Who shall me let?

These were the golden years. The Renaissance came to fruition in the person of the tall handsome young king whom foreign observers, as well as his own subjects, could never praise highly enough. Lord Mountjoy wrote to Erasmus:

> If you could see how everyone here rejoices in having so great a prince, how his life is all their desire, you would not contain yourself for sheer joy. Extortion is put down, liberality scatters riches with a bountiful hand, yet our king does not set his heart on gold or jewels, but on virtue, glory and immortality.

As Wordsworth described a later age:

> Bliss was it in that dawn to be alive,
> But to be young was very heaven!

In this heady excitement of dancing, music, the chase, hectic revels, and courtly ceremonial, the young couple flung themselves with abandon, occasionally with too little inhibition even for bluff King Hal. Wolsey's secretary, Richard Pace, reported to his master in 1517 "Mr. Carew and his wife be returned to the king's grace–too soon in my opinion". What the offence was that earned their joint dismissal is not recorded; some piece of audacity perhaps, an incautious outburst, or some too-free mimicry of the older generation. It was at Christmas time that the revelry reached its peak. The newest form of Italianate entertainment was the masque. The actors spoke their lines behind masks, and wore fantastic costumes; there was music and dancing in which the audience could join while the elaborate set-pieces of scenery were often torn to pieces as a finale. Once the costumes were ripped off as well, by an over-exuberant crowd, leaving the king and his actors in their underclothes. At Greenwich in 1512, a pasteboard castle with gates, towers, artillery and a dungeon was towed into the great hall. Within it were six ladies in russet satin overlaid with gold. Six gallant knights entered and assaulted the castle so valiantly that the ladies relented and led them within, whereupon the castle, La Fortresse Dangerus, crumbled and vanished before their eyes. Two years later, again at Greenwich, four Ladies of Savoy dressed in blue velvet and bonnets of burnished gold were rescued by four gallant knights of Portugal. The strange apparel so delighted the Queen that she invited them to repeat the performance in her bedchamber by torchlight: there were shrieks of merriment when they "put up their visers" and were revealed as Bessie Blount, Elizabeth Carew, and the Ladies Guildford and Fellinger, while the Portuguese knights were seen to be the King, Charles Brandon, Nicholas Carew and Fellinger. A similar performance, with the ladies impersonating Dutch damsels, was presented on Twelfth Night at Eltham Palace; though this time, to avoid scandal, Bessie Blount was replaced by Jane Popyngcourt as partner for the king.

The new year brought excitements of a different sort. War was in the air. Henry bound himself with the Emperor Maxmilian to make an open declaration against King Louis of France. By mid-June the advance guard had disembarked at Calais, where Sir Richard Carew as commander of the castle had already been much involved in preparations. By the end of the month the king himself, with the main force of 11,000 men, arrived in one of the mightiest fleets that England had ever assembled. The army included at least three Carews. Sir Richard, now named as master of the ordonnance, was to lead in the van with a thousand men. Nicholas, as a personal attendant on the king, was part of the King's Ward, while, in the rearguard, a distant cousin from Devon, Sir Edmund Carew, commanded a detachment. With all the panoply of medieval war the army marched out to invest the city of Thérouanne. Following the skirmish often called "the battle of the spurs", Nicholas was awarded a 'coat of rivet' by his royal master, but Sir Edmund died of gunshot wounds and was taken to Calais for burial.

By October, Thérouanne and Tournai had capitulated and the triumphant king was ready to return to England. Nicholas was named as joint lieutenant of Calais with his father, but his duties obviously did not keep him long in France, because at the Christmas revels he and Harry Guildford were issued with twelve yards of yellow sarcenet to make a girdle for the 'mummery'. Amongst the performers were, naturally, Charles Brandon, and 'Maysters Karew the yong wyff'. Thereafter Nicholas played a prominent part in all the ceremonial tournaments which it was Henry's delight to arrange. By 1517 he was knighted, and as keeper of Greenwich Park owned a house convenient for the park and the palace. His time in France was probably used also to perfect his French conversation, because he was frequently employed on embassies to the court of the new king, Francis I, which he found even more extravagant than Henry's own. The chronicler Hall, speaking of one such mission, reported that "Nicholas Carew, Fraunces Brian, and divers other of the young gentlemen of Englande, and thei with the Frenche Kyng roade daily disguysed through the streets of Parish throwing egges, stones, and other foolish trifles at the people, whiche light demeanour of a Kyng was much discommended and gested at. They returne to Englande and are all Frenche in eating, drinking and apparel yea, and in Frenche vices and bragges, so that all the estates of Englande were by them laughed at; the ladies and gentlewomen were dispraised, so that nothyng by them was praised but it were after the Frenche turne."

This was in 1519. As Nicholas had discovered once before, there were limits to the king's good humour beyond which it was inadvisable to tread. One certain way to trouble was to make any unfavourable comparison between the English court and that of Francis I, of whom Henry was jealous beyond all reason. Let Hall continue, "These young minions had been in France and so highly praised the Frenche king and his court, that in a manner they thought little of the King and his court in comparison with the other, they were so high in love with the Frenche court, wherefore their fall was little mourned among wise men."

The Cardinal and the Duke of Norfolk, who rarely saw eye to eye, had joined the other mature members of the privy council in nagging the king to put a stop to the irreverence of "young minions". The French episode decided him to teach them a lesson. They were summoned before the Lord Chamberlain and dismissed their posts. Bryan, Neville and the others were ordered to leave the court while for Nicholas a special punishment was chosen. Guarding the entry to Calais harbour was a lonely fort, the tower of the Rysbanke; to this spot Nicholas found himself promoted lieutenant, and commanded to take up his duties at once. It was a time, says Hall, "sore to him displeasant". There was more than a touch of irony that the man who had praised France should view it from so desolate a spot.

"Then", continues Hall, "was there foure sad and auncient knightes put into the

Kynge's private chamber, whose names were Sir Richard Wingfield, Sir Richard Jernynham, Sir Richard Weston, and Sir William Kyngston: and divers officers were changed in all places." One wonders who was being punished; the sad and auncient knights were at least a guarantee that Carew's banishment would be brief.

From his lonely tower Nicholas had the opportunity to reflect on the ways of Henry Tudor and to ensure that he guarded his tongue in future. Perhaps he dreamed of jousting days at Greenwich, also recorded by Hall, when "the kyng himself, the Duke of Suffolk, the Earl of Essex and Nicholas Carew Esquire took on them to answer all comers. The apparel of the horses was blacke velvet covered all over with branches of Honeysuckles of fine flat gold of damask of loose work, every leaf of the branch moving."

The year had begun well; Nicholas had been appointed sheriff of Surrey and Sussex, and in February the king and court spent a week enjoying the facilities of Nicholas' fine house at Beddington. He had thrown together all the meadowland on either side of the river and enclosed over a hundred acres to create his deer park. On the north side of the enclosure another 200 acres made the 'common park' which ran continuous to Mitcham Common, and Thornton Heath, all of which he owned. In this huge empty area the king might freely indulge his passion for the chase. The king had paid many visits to Croydon, for it was his prerogative to treat the Archbishop's palace as his own. He had wooed Queen Catherine there, and had looked on neighbouring Beddington with its fine park and uncluttered countryside with approval. The emparking took place between 1514 and 1520. It involved exchanges of lands with holders on the site of the new park, notably the Portionist who in 1514 is shown as holding 'Portionary field' but who subsequently exchanged it with Sir Richard Carew for 14 acres in South field (see Pryer pp 24-25). An undated terrier in the Dodd papers shows "Lands which Sir Nicholas Carew holds in his own hands". They include Brakehill and the Little Dovehouse meadow, being *part of the new park* (my italics). It is an interesting speculation that the remains of Bandon village may also have been swept out of existence to clear the way for this visit.

The local people had been working for a year "against the king's coming to Beddington" as a document in the Phillipps Collection puts it. Not least of the problems was the provision of the immense quantities of food and drink that would be consumed during the royal visit. The court rose early on progress and ate little beyond bread, meat, and ale for breakfast, but after a morning passed in hawking, hunting or fishing, they were ready at noon for an immense dinner that must have lasted well into the afternoon. When the king was entertained by the Marquess of Exeter in 1533, the menu listed twenty-nine dishes excluding vegetables. The first course was of salads and cold dishes with such luxuries as stewed sparrows, capons in lemon, and larded pheasant. The main course, served hot, consisted of a great variety of birds: stork, gannet, heron, quail, partridge; as well as fresh sturgeon, venison pasty, and chickens baked in caudle. This was followed by a great variety of sweetmeats, jellies, blancmanges, apples, nuts, clotted cream, quince pie and marchpane which the cooks delighted to mould into fantastic shapes. It was washed down with hippocrass, a spiced wine much loved by the Tudors. Despite the constant exercise Henry was losing the slim figure that he had once boasted.

One wonders whether Sir Richard and Dame Malyn were present with Nicholas and Elizabeth on so important an occasion. The king had need of the special knowledge of the Carews, father and son, for a project that would put into the shade a routine progress dinner.

Cardinal Wolsey planned to make England the arbiter of Europe by staging a summit conference on the borders between France and Calais, and the king was determined that it should outdo in magnificence every similar occurrence that the world had seen. The nobility of England, the Church dignitaries headed by Wolsey and the Archbishop of Canterbury, the queen and the great officers of state, were to assemble at Guisnes on the Calais border. The total English contingent amounted to 5,172 men and women and 2,865 horses. Wolsey's contingent alone included seventy knights as well as his immense household. At Guisnes a palace of wood and painted canvas was to be built to house the participants and provide a background to the feats of arms and gallantry with which it was to be distinguished. In view of all the work that was to be done, the posting of Nicholas to France may be seen as an act of policy rather than a disgrace. Nicholas may have spent less time brooding over his 'displeasant' appointment, than in actively assisting his father in the manifold preparations for the Field of the Cloth of Gold.

Sir Richard died on 18th May, 1520, just three days before Henry set sail from Dover. If worry over the preparations accelerated his death, it had not interfered with his Carew business-sense. His will leaves to Malyn the lands he had lately bought in the county of Guisnes. The rest of his goods, including his harness and arms at Calais and elsewhere, went to Nicholas, including lands at Streatham and in Lincolnshire that had not previously been mentioned as Carew property. He lies in Beddington as his will directs.

The pageantry and martial prowess of the Field of the Cloth of Gold was designed for Nicholas to excel. Even Hall, who disliked him, singles out his costume for description. It was "of white damask embroidered with cloth of gold, a prison with a man looking out with a roll saying in French, "In prison I am at libertye and at libertye I am in prison". The rest of the costume was covered with 'shakles of silver'. Amongst the many ladies serving the French queen, a thirteen-year-old distant cousin of Nicholas watched with approbation, her black eyes sparkling with pleasure at the magnificence of it all. It would be astonishing if either the king or Nicholas had time to spare a glance at Anne Boleyn.

For three weeks the Love feasts, the pageantry, the feats of arms and the shows of amity between the two kings continued in a style never seen before. At the solemn mass conducted by the Cardinal they swore eternal friendship and then returned to their dominions to count the phenomenal cost of the operation and to prepare actively for war.

Nicholas surrendered his lieutenancy on 19th October 1520, and returned to life at court. To serve the king was no sinecure. The gentlemen of the Privy Chamber were organized into two teams of six, each with a nobleman in charge, and one team was always on duty, assisted by two gentlemen ushers, four grooms of the chamber, Penny the royal barber, and a page. The duty team slept on pallets outside the king's door, ready for immediate call. The Household ordinances laid down strict rules to govern their working hours; the Grooms were warned that none should presume "to lay hands upon the royal person, or intermeddle with preparing of dressing of same ... except it be to warm clothes and to hand these to the Gentlemen; both Grooms and Ushers must keep a convenient distance from the king's person, not too homely or bold advancing themselves." All those who served in the king's chamber were enjoined to be "loving together ... and not tattle about such things as may be done or said when the king goes forth, they must leave hearkening and enquiring where the king is or goeth ... not grudging mumbling or talking of the king's pastime, late or early going to bed, or anything done by His Grace." Nor, whilst awaiting the king, must they "use immoderate

13. *The Field of the Cloth of Gold, by an unknown artist*

and continual play, or dice or cards or tables."

They superintended the laying of the royal tables where the rules were even more precise. The panter and the carver were to wear long towels over each shoulder with which they covered their hands before taking up bread, knives, spoons, or the great salt. The carver was to uncover the Salt cellar "and with a cornet of bread touche it in foure partes and with your hand make a flourish over it and give it to the panter to eat for assay." The object was to test for poison, and each dish in turn had to be tested with a flourish before it was served to the king. The rules covered every minute detail; the carver was allowed to steady beef and mutton with his left hand whilst cutting it, but on no account was he to touch venison with his bare hand.

Then, out of the blue, came a shock for those who were intimates of the king. The greatest and proudest of nobles at the court of Henry VIII was Edward, Duke of Buckingham. Through his father, he was descended direct from Thomas Woodstock, the youngest son of Edward III, and through his grandmother, he could, like Henry, trace his descent from John of Gaunt. If there were no Tudor heir he stood next in succession to the throne—he knew it and may in his heart have thought that his claim was better. There had been a foolish quarrel with Wolsey during the Love feast, and, in 1521, he dismissed a servant; the servant repeated to the Cardinal some incautious remarks that he had overheard. The rack and the thumbscrews persuaded others to bear witness against him. Buckingham rode to London without a thought of danger and was bustled immediately to the Tower. On May 13th Nicholas was a member of the jury assembled to hear the testimony of the witnesses. It was not for him to wonder whether idle words were true or false, the king was threatened, and to doubt the evidence would have been that thing which sent icy shudders through him, high treason.

Even the tough old warrior Duke of Norfolk could not hold back the tears as he pronounced sentence of death upon the Duke, and echoes of Buckingham's last words remained in the memory of Nicholas for the rest of his life: "You have said my Lord as a traitor should be spoken to, but I was never one. But, my lords, I nothing malign you for what you have done to me; but the eternal God forgive you my death, and I do. I shall never sue the king for life; howbeit he is a gracious prince, and more grace may come of him than I desire."

If Buckingham, and those who condemned him, believed that the king would relent at the last minute, the hope was never realised. Henry, the good companion, bluff and forthright as they believed him to be, took to his bed with a fever that only cleared when the Duke's head was off.

The execution of Buckingham, although he had never belonged to the circle of intimates, must have shaken those who served the king, though in the predatory atmosphere of the court they did not care to refuse the estates of the dead nobleman. Nicholas received Blechingley in the share-out. The years that followed were busy and they brought many new honours, Constable of Wallingford Castle and Steward of Brasted Manor; and in 1522 he became the king's Master of Horse. The Tudor court was ever restlessly on the move. Eltham, Greenwich, Bridewell, Richmond, Windsor, Woodstock; and, during the summer months when plague was endemic in London, they travelled further afield on progress to the houses of the greater subjects. The change of scene was partly a matter of provisioning. The state of the roads was such that it was easier to move people than the great quantities of food consumed by the army of attendants, officials, courtiers, guards, cooks, armourers, locksmiths, laundresses, petitioners, and hangers-on, who, with their wives, mistresses, and personal servants, claimed a right to eat at the king's table. It was also partly a matter of sanitation. Though the greater palaces were all by the Thames, and incorporated a system of sewers down to the river, the great numbers of people, the rush-strewn floors, and untidy Tudor habits, made a great risk of epidemic amongst them. As Master of the Horse, it became Nicholas's task, with a staff of sixty men, to organise transport whenever the court was on the move. It was an office of high importance, that a generation later the great Earl of Leicester was to perform for Elizabeth.

In 1527 he was sent again on an embassy to France, and in the following year served once more as Sheriff of Surrey and Sussex, a post which perhaps allowed him some time to enjoy his "fair house" at Beddington that Thomas Fuller said "by the advantage of the water is a paradise of pleasure". Embassies were frequent in these years; Francis Bryan was sent to Rome, and in the autumn of 1529 Nicholas went on a six month mission to the Emperor Charles V at Bologna. There is no doubt about the purpose, for the 'King's great matter' was coming to a head. Henry was petulantly in love with Anne Boleyn and had persuaded himself that the failure of his queen to give him a male heir was evidence of Divine displeasure at the incestuous relationship into which he had been trapped. When Nicholas returned in February it was to find that Wolsey had been deprived of the Chancellorship and had retired to Esher.

In this year Nicholas, more successful than his master, became father of an heir. The child was christened Francis, probably as a compliment to his uncle; Nicholas was still in high favour with Henry who judged that he had done well on his various embassies, and, in February 1531, the king came again to Beddington, probably bringing in his train Anne Boleyn, soon to become his queen. A charming, but certainly false, local legend tells that as the cavalcade passed by Carshalton church her charger reared up, its hooves kicking up a tiny spring which ever afterwards received her name. Anne Boleyn's well is dry now, but a modern statue of the unfortunate lady stands on the nearby almshouses watching the spot.

Henry doubtless admired again the fine deer park, and noted the improvements which Nicholas had made to the house since his last visit, and the fine table-tomb that he had provided for his father in the Carew Chapel. The king was now furiously impatient to be wedded to his new love, and in defiance of convention they often rode abroad with Nicholas as the sole attendant. The estates had been enlarged—Banstead, with its wide expanses of downland, was rented from Queen Catherine and was soon to be his, outright. Ravensbury, to the north, he had purchased from the Duke of Suffolk, and he now controlled a continuous territory from Streatham to Blechingley.

The following year Nicholas was again ordered to France, this time to arrange a meeting for Henry with Francis I; but it was no longer the thoughtless headstrong youth with round face in the engraving reproduced by Lysons, who travelled to Paris. He had grown lean with the passing years, and was finding his loyalties gravely stretched. Though Anne was a distant cousin, and though the pro-French party to which he had always belonged was thought to be against the Spanish queen, he confessed privately to Chapuys, the emperor's ambassador, that he was travelling to France to advance her claims sorely against his will. In this very year Sir Thomas More had resigned the Chancellorship rather than acknowledge Henry as head of the English church, and, though formal religion meant little to Nicholas, his conscience was uneasy. Anne's imperious temper had already estranged his friends Harry Guildford and

Charles Brandon. King Francis received him well, Nicholas found the atmosphere of the French Court relaxing after the tensions around Henry, and the French king had many times requested that Nicholas should be granted new honours.

In 1533 Anne Boleyn was crowned queen and Nicholas was appointed her champion, to ride fully armed at her coronation feast, offering to give battle on her behalf to any who dared to challenge her title. In this year, too, Francis I wrote to Henry asking that the Order of the Garter should be conferred upon Nicholas, and, in the following year, that he should be made Chancellor of the Order. Henry replied briefly that the Chancellorship was already bestowed upon the King of Scotland.

Other duties came his way; Chapuys records that in July 1535 someone tampered with the king's fool, "ung Innocent", and taught him to say that the queen was "Une ribalde" and her child a bastard. The king was in such a fury that the fool's life was in danger, and Nicholas Carew hustled him away until the royal rage had abated. The king, caught between a shrewish wife, a tender conscience, and an ulcerated leg, was developing the uncertain and terrible temper of his later years. During Anne's brief reign there was an attempt to force the Princess Mary to renounce both her faith and her legitimacy, and those about the king were caught up in the conflict of wills. Francis Bryan and Anthony Browne were held for questioning, while Exeter, Carew's superior, was ordered not to come to the council. The tension became intolerable. When it was all over, and Mary, in response to pleas from Nicholas and Elizabeth Carew, as well as everyone else who felt sympathy for the unfortunate girl, had submitted, Henry once more became 'bluff King Hal' and wagged a genial forefinger at Bryan, exclaiming "Ah is me. Naughty bruits are soon blown." Yet all those about him knew that 'naughty bruits' could have ended all too easily upon Tower Hill.

Nicholas had struck up a friendship with a young knight, Sir Edward Seymour, who had newly been promoted Gentleman of the Privy Chamber, and whose sister Jane, a maid of honour to the queen, had already caught Henry's wandering eye. Carew's wordly wisdom, and his long knowledge of the king, was useful to the inexperienced girl. In a court where Chapuys said it was hard for any Englishwoman to remain a virgin for long, Nicholas and her brother impressed upon her that the most certain way to the king's heart and a crown was to hold him off. Jane learned her lesson well, and just three years after Nicholas had offered to do battle with the world on behalf of Anne Boleyn, he became the unofficial guardian of her rival. Anne's brief reign was almost over, but she had yet to face a jury who would find her guilty of adultery. Few mourned her passing; but in order that all legal niceties might be tied up, the king removed to Hampton in order that he might not influence the court, and modest, gentle, Jane Seymour was taken out of the public eye, probably to the obscurity of Beddington.

Charged with Queen Anne in the Tower were Lord Rochford, her brother; Henry Norris, and Francis Weston, all gentlemen of the Privy Chamber and drinking and jousting companions of Nicholas. Sir Francis Bryan might have made one of their number had not some word of warning or timely intuition caused him to pick a quarrel with Lord Rochford and so break loose from the faction.

The king soon found Beddington an impossible distance from the woman whom he adored, and Nicholas had perforce to find lodgings for Jane in the village of Hampton. Thither came Francis Bryan with the expected news that the queen and all those arrested with her were to die. It is hard to imagine Thomas Cromwell being shocked by callous behaviour, but the adroit change of sides and the manner of his communication of the death sentence earned for Bryan the nickname "The Vicar of Hell". Henry celebrated the news with a pageant on the river and in the evening went off to sup with Jane at her lodgings. "You never saw prince nor man make greater show of his horns, nor show them more pleasantly" wrote Chapuys.

The new queen brought relief to the dark mood of the court. In the joy of his bride Henry forgot the pain in his leg and "useth himself more like a good fellow than a king". To the gentlemen of the Privy Chamber it was like a return to the carefree days that were so long past. The closure of the monastries, the burning of protestants, and the hanging of catholics, only meant richer pickings for those who were nearest to him. It was the time when the Carew estates burgeoned to their greatest extent. The closure of the Abbey at Chertsey brought Nicholas the manors of Sutton, Epsom, Coulsdon and Horley. There was no landowner in the eastern part of Surrey who could match him in estates or in wealth.

The birth in 1537 of the long-hoped-for heir to the throne was marred only by the death of the gentle queen. At the elaborate and lengthy christening ceremony of Prince Edward, Nicholas with three others "in aprons and towels, took charge of the font and kept same until they were discharged thereof by the Lord Steward or Treasurer of the King's House in his absence".

If Nicholas and his friends sometimes felt they were walking a tightrope, they must have speculated with friends, and amongst themselves, when it would end; when would the moment come that they should leap off to safety to a post, perhaps in Ireland, away from the dangers of the centre; dare they preserve the delicate balance that paid so richly and so dangerously? Nicholas hoped that his friendship with Edward Seymour, the next king's uncle, would bring the ultimate reward, a barony or an earldom. Meanwhile there were times for those about the king when the tension was all but intolerable. "He will die one day, suddenly," declared Lord Montague, "His leg will kill him and then we shall have jolly stirring." This was dangerous talk, there were servants paid to listen and report such things in every great household. Others were more circumspect, they talked about "a change in the world".

In November 1538 the Marquis of Exeter and Lord Montague were suddenly arrested: both had Plantagenet blood in their veins; Exeter was the king's first cousin. It was said that he had looked sad when news was brought to him that Henry had an heir. Both had talked incautiously in their time; in their background lurked that assiduous weaver of dis-affection, the Imperial ambassador Chapuys. It was absurd, however, to say as Wriothesley did of Exeter, "A traitor these twenty years, he ever studies to take his master's place from him." It was like the case of Buckingham all over again. The grim farce of interrogation, collecting of statements, questioning of servants, torturing of lesser suspects, dragged in new people as they became implicated. While all those who had ever known them held their breath, and waited. Sir Edward Neville was taken; so was Montague's elderly mother, the Countess of Salisbury. Carew burnt correspondence; Exeter had been his superior in the Privy Chamber, he could not change sides over that. The execution of those accused was certain though the Countess was reserved to die at a later date. The survivors breathed more easily. Yet Henry was so sure of himself that he could play with his next victims as a cat does a mouse. Thomas Fuller quotes the family tradition of how the end came for Nicholas: "King Henry then at bowls gave this knight opprobious language, betwixt jest and earnest; to which the other returned an answer rather true than discrete as more consulting therein his own animosity than allegiance. The king who in this kind would give but would not take, being no good fellow in tart repartees, was so highly offended thereat that Sir Nicholas fell from the top of his favour to the bottom of his displeasure, and was bruised to death thereby."

Could a single hasty answer doom a favourite of nearly thirty years standing? Or was the quarrel a device to bring about something that was already determined? Nicholas was arrested on 14th February 1539. He was charged as an accomplice of the Marquis of Exeter "knowing the said Marquis to be a traitor, in order to keep him in his traitorous intentions . . . had conversations with him about the change of the world and also with his own hand wrote him divers letters, at Bedyngton . . . and the said Marquis . . . sent divers traitorous letters to the said Carew . . . which letters they afterwards to conceal their treason, traitorously burnt." It was further reported that when he heard of the indictment of Exeter, "He traitorously said these words, 'I marvel greatly that the indictment against the Lord Marquis was so secretly handled, and for what purpose the like was never seen.' "

At his interrogation he was asked to give details of letters he had written to the Marquis and to the Lady Marquis, whether they were signed, and if not why not. He was asked what he had written touching the king and the late princess dowager, or the Lady Mary, or of the king's proceedings with Sir Edward Neville or with Lord Montague. Testimony against him was given by a servant of Catherine of Aragon–it was largely irrelevant. Sir Nicholas, he said, wrote no letters to the ex-queen, but his wife did write to her. He had written, however, to the Lady Mary urging her to accept the king's judgement, but saying "I did give my heart to her for her mother's sake". The letter that was described was perfectly loyal and contained such sentiments as "he was sure that Master Secretary would give a hundred pounds that she would consent to do the king's bidding." Lady Carew had written to Mary in similar terms.

Chapuys reported to his master that the grand Escuyer, Master Caro was taken prisoner to the Tower and that the moment his arrest was ordered, commissioners went out to seize all his goods in his houses. "It is presumed that the King will not have forgotten to charge them to take the most beautiful diamonds and pearls and innumerable jewels which he formerly gave to the said Escuyer's wife, the greater part of which he had taken from the late good Queen." Chapuys, quoting from current rumour, said that a letter from Nicholas had been found in the coffer of the Marchioness of Exeter, and that when Carew took the news of the birth of a prince to Exeter that the Marquis 'Looked sad'. He concluded with the belief that the devotion of Nicholas to the Lady Mary was the true cause of his fall. "The said Escuyer has always shown himself a most devoted servant. It would seem that they wish to leave her as few such as possible."

CHAPTER FIVE

The Death of a Carew

O N THE morning of March 3rd 1539, Nicholas Carew was conducted from the Tower to die. The scene was grimly familiar; the low grass-covered hill crossed by footpaths ringed about by leaning timber and plaster houses; the spire of the city's oldest church, All Hallows; the foetid moat that received all the filth from the city ditch and was only renewed by the ebb and flow of the tide; the snarl of the lions in the Tower menagerie near the gates; the grey walls that he was leaving for ever; the curious, but not hostile, crowds, and, in the centre, erected for the occasion, the scaffold.

More than a fortnight had passed since his examination before the Council and he was prepared for death. His jailer, Thomas Phillips, had brought him a copy of a newly translated book; it was the Bible in English and with the shadow of death upon him he had read with trembling curiosity. He had, no doubt, been visited by Elizabeth and the children on the night before. Perhaps his mother, Dame Malyn, who was to outlive him by another five years, came too. There was little he could say to console them: the property of a condemned traitor reverted to the king, there would be nothing for his son, nine year old Francis, to inherit, and no marriage portions for his daughters. Perhaps an appeal to Thomas Cromwell might save something for them. There was no one else who would dare to risk the king's displeasure for the sake of a widow and her children. The companions with whom he had drunk and diced and jousted were already greedily selecting the manors for which they would sue; had he not done likewise?

He had passed many hours preparing the speech that he would deliver from the scaffold. It was to be his last public appearance and he hoped that his words would be remembered. He had written out the speech in full and a copy came through Sir Robert Chester to Archbishop Parker and is amongst the manuscripts of Corpus Christi College, Cambridge. The little cortège of halbardiers; Nicholas; the priest bearing a crucifix; and the Lieutenant of the Tower, took several minutes to reach the platform where the masked headsman waited by the block, the axe discreetly laid aside in the straw. A group of gallants stood by the ladder. Nicholas knew them all, but they turned their eyes away in embarrassment; as he climbed the ladder he could see others taking a grandstand view from the windows of the nearby houses. The halbardiers made a ring about the scaffold, he looked over their heads at the waiting crowds; it was to them that he would speak. "Farewell my masters," he began, "I thank you all for your coming hither at this instant, trusting that ye be not come only to see me die, but also to lift up your hands to Almighty God as I shall most heartily desire you when you shall see the axe divide my head and body asunder, so that at your humble petition He will vouchsafe to call my soul to everlasting salvation. And that I may have Grace in spirit I ask you to cry 'Mercy, mercy, mercy.' " He cast nervousness aside as he came to his message, he could see lips framing 'mercy' already. "I most humbly thank the King's Majesty for that respite of time that he hath suffered me to live in yonder prison since the time of my first committing, whereby I have exercised myself in the reading of the Old Testament and the New. By the Old I have found great and bitter menace and threat and by the New all hope and most comfortable words as thus 'Come unto me all ye that be heavily laden and I will refresh you. Knock and it shall be opened to you.' I humbly thank my Lord God that reading I have knocked and have found his grace opened unto me. And I, wretched man, heavily laden with the burden of sin have from the bottom of my heart even called on him and he hath refreshed me so that I stand in firm hope of everlasting salvation and so trust that this night I shall rest amongst the elect of God through the merit of Christ's passion, my Saviour and Redeemer."

There were murmurs of sympathy amongst the crowd. There were always those who wept easily at this spectacle. This was living drama, the stuff of tragedy, with real noblemen to play the parts and real blood. They loved it as they wept. He went on; "Therefore I shall exhort you all that can read to read those Holy Scriptures and so many of you as cannot read that you will resort to those that can read unto you, assuring you that thereby you shall learn the right duty of Christian men towards God and also learn to lead the rest of your lives in all Godly honesty and comeliness with the reward of Eternal Life if you truly observe the same. And now I must confess unto you that I as a reprobate, before this my committing, could never find it in my hearrt to read any book of Scripture; nor could I well brook, but rather malign such as had any good will thereunto. Therefore I verily beseech that if you had called me out of this life by any other means than this I had gone to the devil both body and soul without redemption."

Though the king was not present it was important to say all the right things, for there were those listening who would give a full report, and the right word might save something for Elizabeth and the children. "And now I have further to move you" he continued, "that ye make intercession from the bottom of your hearts to Almighty God for the prosperous preservation of the King's majesty, your most natural and liege sovereign lord that he through your prayers may have long life and reign over you. And I do wish in God that you and all the rest of his good subjects did so well know him as I do, for that I have been brought up under His Majesty since I was six years old. During that time I must say as duty moveth me how far his excellence, his comely person, his approved valiantness, with aptness to all feats of arms, his skill, that lively nature, his princely liberality to all such as have served him faithfully, that he the most worthy is to be elected your King and Governor." He remembered wry smiles on similar occasions and added quickly, "You may not take me to say this as a flatterer or as one who hopes to have life for I know the end thereof is at hand." He had a few coals of fire for those of his drinking companions who stood now, aloof and for the moment safe. "And now I beseech you to pray with me for the prosperity and life of those men of worship which passed in trial of my life and death, for they upon the evidence to them given have done to me as, if I had been one of them, and one of them as I am, I would have done the like. But yet they were but men like myself; they could not judge the inward man, but Almighty God when he shall come in Glory to judge the whole world it shall be made clear to all and he shall manifest it that I do suffer death here this day as firm a subject to my liege sovereign Lord as any that liveth or shall live after me. And thus I end trusting that ye will not forget my first prayer made unto you."

He turned towards the block, removing his cloak to expose his neck. The executioner went on one knee before him and mumbled the formal request for forgiveness while offering the bandage with which to cover his eyes. Carew put aside the cloth. "God forgive thee, and I do" he said "but to blindfold me it shall not need."

His body lies with that of Elizabeth his wife, in St. Botolph's Church, Aldgate, and we will let Thomas Fuller speak the last word about him. "He was a jolly gentleman."

There is another reason why Nicholas Carew had to die. Henry was getting old; his ulcerated leg not only ruined his temper, but made travelling difficult. In 1538 he had completed the purchase of the manor of Cuddington, and, having razed to the ground the church and village, began the erection of the palace that was to be called Nonsuch. He already owned great tracts of the Surrey countryside. His palaces at Richmond (Sheen) and at Weybridge (Oatlands) included large hunting parks. Windsor Great Park extended deep into Surrey and abutted the agriculturally useless lands around Bagshot. Lands formerly held by Wolsey stretched south of the Thames from Hampton Court, and almost joined the new estates of Cuddington, Ewell, and Cheam and Worcester Park. We know that he had already had a dream of making the whole county subject to Forest Law so that he could indulge his passion for the chase untrammelled by the rights of local landowners, and with a sufficiency of hunting boxes scattered across the area where he might expect entertainment.

In furtherance of this ambition, the Carew empire would place the greater part of the county within his grasp. It is true that in 1538 Nicholas received great tracts of land that had formerly belonged to the Abbey of Chertsey. They included Sutton, Epsom, Coulsdon and Horley but it was one of the nastier traits of his royal master to build up the hopes of the victim that he had already determined to destroy. The death of Carew had little to do with Exeter, and nothing to do with bowls, it was his lands that Henry coveted, the rest followed naturally.

Nine days after the execution Elizabeth Carew wrote to Thomas Cromwell. The letter was addressed from Wallington where the widow had taken refuge after being evicted from the great house at Beddington. In the eyes of most biographers, Cromwell is the evil genius behind Henry's throne, but this is not how he was seen by contemporaries. Immensely able and industrious, and the man nearest to the king, he was the person most likely to intercede for the widow and children of an executed traitor. Though the Carews doubtless despised and in private mocked at his humble origins (sure proof of his ability), and perhaps because of them, they felt free to make their appeals direct to him.

Elizabeth wrote "In most humblest wise I beseech your Lordship to be a good lord to me and my poore children, and take a medyator unto the King's Grace for me for my lyving and my childrens. And that your lordship will speake to hys Grace that I may enjoy that which hys Grace gave me which is Bletchingley and Wallyngton, trusting that hys Grace will not give hit from me, and I humbly desyre your good lordship to speke a good word to hys Grace for me that I may enjoy hit according to hys Graces graunt. And advertise your lordship I have but twentie pound more of my husbands landis which is small joynter."

Her request was reinforced by her mother, garrulous Lady Bryan, nurse to the infant Prince Edward, and accustomed to pouring out her troubles about underclothes and infant teeth in long rambling letters to the Secretary. She begged Cromwell to show kindness to "my poor daughter Carew, there is no house she can lie in and I beg that she may have Becherynlie which his Grace gave her without asking. She has not been used to straight living and it would grieve me in my old days to lose her."

The plea of mother and daughter was not granted. Cromwell had troubles of his own to surmount. He was arranging yet another royal marriage made possible by the death of Jane Seymour, a union with Anne of Cleves. It was to cause the downfall of Master Secretary. The king took an instant dislike to the "Flanders mare" and having first created him Earl of Essex, destroyed him. The manor of Blechingley, and of Walton on the Hill, were going to be needed, along with other estates, as Anne's price for a quiet annulment of the marriage. Elizabeth Carew was allowed to retain Wallington and a group of Sussex manors around Plumpton and Barcombe.

Meanwhile the house at Beddington was put under the charge of Sir Michael Stanhope who was ordered to prepare an inventory of the goods and chattels. Amongst the books were the rolls of the manor, the chronicles of Froissart and a hand-drawn and illuminated book in parchment, lined with gold of "Confessio Amantis" by Gower. The estates in Surrey were incorporated with those of Nonsuch, Oatlands and Hampton Court into the Honour of Hampton Court. Each property was managed by a king's officer who acted as steward, or bailiff, while a clause inserted into the Act of Annexation gave some safeguard to holders of adjacent manors which were not incorporated.

Lady Malyn, the mother of Nicholas, (her name is given as Maude in the relevant papers) continued to live in Beddington, perhaps in the building later to be called the Old Post Office. She was to suffer still more grief in 1539. The Rector of Beddington, Charles Carew, was an illegitimate son of Nicholas. In addition to the profits of his parish he received those tithes due to the Portioner, and had been installed as the master of Lovekyn's Chapel at Kingston. Using a servant of the old lady's, and two of his own as the agents, he conspired to rob his grandmother of her money, plate and rings "to her utter undoing." The goods were recovered except for eight pounds in money, and under the brutal interrogation of the time he confessed to the crime. Amongst Cromwell's papers is a letter of thanks from Malyn. "If I had my sight" she wrote, "I would have waited on you to thank you, but my son Sir Arthur Darcy, has shown me your great kindness. I ask you to be a mean to the King to have pity on the offenders. Considering how near I am to the pit . . . I think that my conscience will not be discharged and that my life will be shorter unless I persuade you to my inward intent." Charles Carew was one of those who died by the rope and the hangman's knife in a mass execution in August 1540.* Cromwell himself two days before.

After years of living a life that was, in the words of Machiavelli, "rich, ferocious and greedy for glory" it may have been a relief for Elizabeth Carew to withdraw with her children into retirement. She did not, apparently, follow the usual course of bereaved wives at this time and marry again. There is no record of the birth of her children, but five: four daughters and a son, Francis, survived the dangers of infancy. Of the

---

* There has been great confusion over this incident. A commission set up under Elizabeth I failed to find any reason for the death of Charles Carew. The compilers of VCH said that it was Elizabeth, the widow of Nicholas who suffered the loss, yet correctly said the letter written on 20th November 1539 was from Maude. Unfortunately Malyn herself added to the confusion by calling Sir Arthur Darcy her 'son' when he was in fact the husband of her granddaughter. The matter has been cleared by Mrs. Richardson's persistence with the State Papers.

daughters, Isabel married Nicholas Saunder of Ewell, from a family of yeoman origins with whom the Carews had several links; their son, also named Nicholas, was knighted by Queen Elizabeth. Mary, the third daughter, married Sir Arthur Darcy, third son of Lord Darcy. There is a breath of convenience about this, because Lord Darcy was the last to receive the grant of Beddington before its restoration to the Carews, and his son received Sutton and Epsom as a marriage settlement. The youngest child, Anne Carew, whose story is relevant to this account, married a rising young diplomat, a friend of the Seymours and of Catherine Parr, Sir Nicholas Throckmorton. While the Throckmortons pursued the excitements, and dangers, of life at court, Francis Carew was taken into the service of Mary Tudor. There was little else that Mary could do for the son of a man who had died because he was her friend. During the reign of her brother Mary spent most of her time at Kenninghall, a manor furthest removed from London. His service held small prospect of advancement for Francis, the best that Mary could hope for at that time was marriage to an obscure foreign prince, the worst that she feared was death at the hands of the protestants.

Yet, she was a Tudor, and when summoned to London in 1550 she rode in state along Cheapside with fifty gentlemen in front and eighty ladies and gentlemen behind, all ostentatiously carrying their forbidden rosaries. It was an act of defiance that Francis, aged twenty, probably found exciting. Equally exciting, and even more dangerous, three years later, was her progress towards London to the sickbed of her brother; when she was stopped at Hoddesdon with the news that the king was dead, and Lady Jane Grey proclaimed queen. The messenger who brought the news to warn her of danger had been sent by Sir Nicholas Throckmorton. Nine days later the situation was reversed, Northumberland was arrested and Mary was queen.

In January 1554 the new queen issued an order to her attorney general, "We are pleased and contented that Francis Carewe Escuyer sonne and heire of Sir Nicholas Carewe deceased shall have in gift of us to hym and to his heires forever in Fee simple the manors of Beddington, Ravensdon, Bandon and Norbury in the County of Surrey and all other lands houses and heridytaments in the same county . . . also . . . the manours of Ebbysham (Epsom) and Sutton . . . and the manours of Bansted and Walton on the Hill with lands in Charlewood and Horley". Other lands were in Kent, Sussex, Northumberland and Lincoln. So the Carews returned to Beddington, but not immediately; for Francis prudently went through a form of purchase from Lord Darcy before he took possession. What the queen gave another might take away. Elizabeth Carew did not live to see these happier days. She had made her will at Wallington in 1541, but it was not proven until 1546 when it is assumed she died. She had little to leave beyond her wearing apparel to Lady Darcy, £40 to her daughter Isabel; and remembrances to her brother Francis, to Arthur Darcy, her brother-in-law, and to Lady Bryan, her mother. She lies with her husband in St. Botolph's, Aldgate.

The seesaw of events that brought Francis back to Beddington proved near disastrous for his brother-in-law. Throckmorton's protestantism made him suspect and in spite of the timely warning that had probably saved Mary for her throne, he was caught up in the aftermath of Sir Thomas Wyatt's rebellion, and found himself facing a court, charged with High Treason. The court had already condemned Lady Jane Grey and Wyatt himself, and others who had certainly aided him. No one before had ever escaped from this, the most dread of all charges. Nicholas Throckmorton made legal history by talking his way out of the death penalty. He was returned to the Tower, where

14. Sir Nicholas Throckmorton, brother-in-law of Sir Francis Carew

he was joined by the jurors who had acquitted him. The company was good, other prisoners included Robert Dudley, one day to become the Earl of Leicester; and the Lady Elizabeth, the next queen.

Sir Nicholas Throckmorton obtained his release when Mary's short reign was over and spent the rest of his life in the service of her sister. The early days of the reign were passed as the trusted ambassador to the court of France. In the later years he was employed in a number of delicate missions to Mary Queen of Scots; so delicate indeed that towards the end of his life he was in some danger of being caught up in the many plots to free that unfortunate lady.

CHAPTER SIX

Sir Francis Carew, Country Gentleman

S IR FRANCIS CAREW, (he was knighted before 1587), never married, but his great
house with its thirty-five servants can never have been a lonely place. The names of many
of his staff occur in the accounts prepared by his steward, Thomas Mabson, which are
printed in Bentham's little History of Beddington. There were the men-servants,
Hughson, Holburne, Adams, Ellis, Tegge and Rogers with perhaps the boy who always
appeared by his christian name of Nicholas. Their wages, like Mabson's, varied between
thirty shillings and twenty shillings per annum but they must have eaten in the house and
they all received additional payments for other services. The wife of one, Mrs. Tegge, the
housekeeper, received £2 per annum. The daily labourers who did much of the
maintenance about the estates received 8d. a day when they worked.

Richard Elmer, the blacksmith, made up an account for many items that were home
produced. He made many nails of various types to "nayle ye great tubbe in the
bruhouse"; to mend the pigeon house gate and a bench in the milk house. He made a
hinge for the oat tub, a shovel for the kitchen, a cleaver to cleave mutton with, and a "fyer
panne for ye parlour". He mended a gun for 'Ric' and did many other repairs to fire-arms
as well as making lynch pins for cartwheels and "dragges for the oxen".

Thomas Mabson collected rents from the tenants at 'Egebridge' (Hackbridge),
Beddington, Bandon, Waddon and Woodcote. He received the threepences which the
villagers paid as rent for their cottages and gardens (they paid an extra penny for each
other dependant that lived with them). Others for whom he accounted held outlying
farms and lands at Portnalls (Coulsdon) Bristoonham (?), a close at Mitcham, and a
house and lands at Brighton (sic). At Easter time the various goodwives of the village,
Goode Nedell, Goode Mant, and nine others, turned up with the traditional baskets of
eggs and poultry.

A Dovecote, probably later than that for which Richard Elmer repaired the gate,
stands alongside the manor. It has spaces within for 1,000 nests and a circular ladder by
which the nests could be raided for eggs and squabs. The range of cottages which extend
from it down towards the river probably housed the labourers, and perhaps also included
the brewhouse, milk house, hawk mews, and stables which are also mentioned in the
accounts. The great barns and cowhouses must have stood elsewhere, perhaps in the
village centre where in the nineteenth century Manor farm was to be found.

The deer park that had been enclosed by Sir Nicholas stretched to the west and
north of the manor house, covering a larger area than the present Beddington Park. Sir
Francis would have been unique amongst his contemporaries if he had not enjoyed the

16. *Outbuildings, Carew Manor, in 1951*

15. *The Dovecote*

thrill of the chase, but hunting in Tudor times was more than an agreeable exercise, it was an essential way of providing the large meals of fresh meat that were customarily consumed. The river curves through the park and Sir Francis carried out works with it that were to delight his contemporaries as well as later ages. Behind the house the water entered the grounds by a cascade that was only removed a few years ago; the river then formed a large tee-shaped lake in the garden. A spring from the higher ground to the south supplied the moat from which a channel already referred to brought running water to the kitchen basement-room. The water flowed from the moat into another ornamental water stretching a full hundred metres in front of the house. The depression in which this lake lay can still be seen between the avenue of chestnut trees. Somewhere within the garden a waterwheel drove a pump that supplied fresh water to the house. The supply of fresh water may have prompted the installation of the water closet that so intrigued John Aubrey a century later; "Here I saw a pretty machine to cleanse the House of Office viz by a small Stream, no bigger than one's finger which ran into an Engine made like a bit of a Fire-shovel, which hung upon its center of Gravity; so that when it was full, a considerable Quantity of Water fell down with some Force, and washed away the Filth." Sir John Harrington, the inventor of this useful novelty, owned the Manor of Wallington briefly and one wonders whether Sir Francis picked up the idea in conversation with him.

The river, of course, also received and carried away the household sewage, but with fewer than a hundred people about the house and estate, and perhaps another two hundred in the parish, pollution was hardly a problem. The sewers by which it was conveyed are largely responsible for the stories of secret passages that are still sometimes told about the house.

Only the great hall and the cellars at either end have survived unaltered since the time of Sir Francis Carew. The house was rebuilt in c1710 and again between 1859 and 1866. The first rebuilding was engraved by Colen Campbell in 1715 with a plan that suggests that the baroque appearance was only a facelift given to the central portion of the house which remained substantially unaltered, at least in plan. There were ten rooms in this part and they match up well with an incomplete inventory that was made in the year 1596. But this was only part of the great mansion that entertained three sovereigns and in 1663 paid 'hearth tax' for fifty chimneys. Thomas Fuller writing at the same time called the building 'a palace'. There can be no doubt that under Sir Francis the building achieved a greater size and a magnificence than it would ever know again.

The inventory shows the hall to have been sparsely furnished, the principal living room being the 'Parler' at its north end. In this room there was a long table covered by a green 'carpet' and ten 'joyned Stoules' and two leather chairs. There was a square table, also covered by green carpet and a 'court coubberd with tow drawers and lockes to them'. There were many 'couchins' some in 'Yallow' and 'orindgetauny needelwork', others in green or red velvet and some in leather. The walls were coverd with 'wenscot' and hung with painted cloths. The most valuable articles in the room were three 'olde turki carpets' and two new ones valued at £6 11s. 0d. compared with 6s. 8d. for 18 pictures. 'A payre of virginals stood in this room, a reminder of the Elizabethan love of music. Visiting royalty slept in the room above, 'the great chamber' in a 'bedsted' valued at three shillings, but as woodwork was probably done on the estate it was little regarded. It sounds comfortable enough, having a 'downe featherbed with a bolster and two downe pillows worth £5 6s. 8d. On the featherbed were two blankets and a counterpane of tapestry worth £5. The bed had '5 curtins of crimosin wosted and one vallence of needelwork with crimosin silk fringe'. Apart from the fire-irons there was no other furniture in this room except for a 'crimosin satin cheayre' and two long cushions one of them 'payned with velvet and cloth of gold and lined with purpel caffa'. Six other bed chambers are listed. The furnishings were less grand, though even the maid's chamber had two bedsteads with featherbeds, bolsters, two blankets and a red coverlet; they also contained two spinning wheels. The servants' chamber was similarly provided and had in it 'a tow handed sworde' that someone had put in there and forgotten.

The kitchen, a separate block at the south end of the hall, retained its Elizabethan appearance until the 1865 rebuilding as may be seen in a drawing c1820 by Joseph Nash. It comprised a hall, approximately 33 by 16 feet, open to the roof timbers with a huge fire place at one end. On one side of the hearth brick steps went down to the semi-basement already referred to, and, on the other, a narrow staircase led up to the kitchen chamber above. At the lower end an addition (at least in 1715) provided the 'house of office' for which the inventory lists

a wenscote pres, a close stoole with a frame, an olde wicker cheayre and a scrine.

It is in keeping with other plans of the period to suppose that in front of the mansion was an enclosed court rather wider than the present quadrangle that compromised additional servants' quarters, perhaps a lodging for Mabson, a stable for riding horses, and the servants' privies. Opposite to the entrance of the hall would be the gatehouse and drawbridge giving access across the moat to the park.

Thomas Mabson's accounts include what he calls 'a boke for your servants akate'* which is an itemised list of food consumed by the household week by week. The number of people who ate in the house is not given, but they drank a barrel of beer each week and consumed twenty loaves and 'a mutton'; presumably a whole sheep. Some weeks they also had beef, 'vij pese' or 'a capon iij chakens' several pounds of butter and cheese and four or five eggs. They ate a great deal of fish, itemised in two entries to correspond to the two compulsory fish days of Wednesday and Friday. The twenty-five herrings eaten on each day may be the number of people fed, but they also ate two and a half 'fyshe': probably salt cod.

The Mabson accounts date from 1569 and by a curious chance another household book of the Carew estates dating from 1607 survived in the possession of Sir Henry Lambert. This was kept by Mabson's successor, William Blake, and lists principally the items purchased outside the estate, giving aspects of life during the year. The servants are listed by name; there are now 35 of them, of whom the four top men receive 25 shillings each half year; they include William Joanes, the gardener. Labourers continue to be paid at a rate of eight pence a day and women at half that rate; but skilled men, the mason and the carpenter, receive one shilling and two pence a day; the plumber has a shilling, with eightpence paid out for his lodging; while one, John Shirlock, has one shilling and fourpence a day for working in the 'figg house'.

At the beginning of November, before rains made the roads difficult, the household laid-in the supplies of fish that would have to last through the winter; so we read:

Item Nicholas Parker for carryage of iii basketts to London and
bringing whome a load of fish   vs vjd (5s. 6d.)

* Note: "akate", an obsolete word, spelt "Cates" in the later account, derives from the French "acheter" i.e. the items bought.

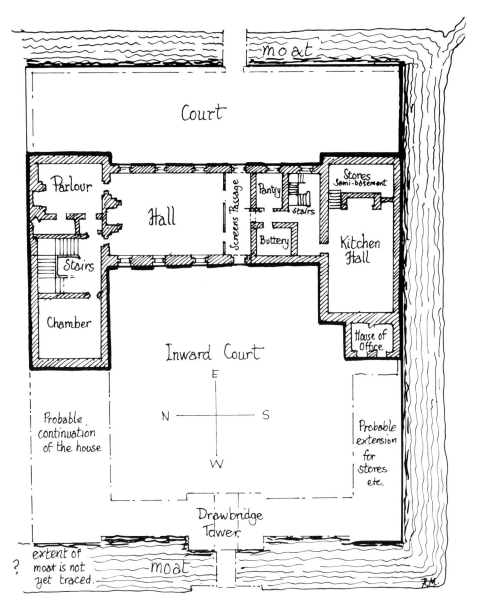

moat

Court

Parlour

Hall

Screens Passage

Pantry

stairs

Stores
Semi-basement

Stairs

Buttery

Kitchen
Hall

Chamber

Inward Court

E

N — S

W

Probable
continuation
of the house

Probable
extension
for
stores
etc.

House of
Office

Drawbridge
Tower.

? extent of
moat is not
yet traced.

moat

17. Plan of the house in the time of Sir Francis Carew, based on a plan of 1715 and an inventory of 1596

Five and sixpence was a lot of money at a time when a labourer received eightpence a day, but the twenty mile round trip would take two days at least and the payment would therefore include food and stabling for his horses as well as a night's lodging for Parker. On checking the baskets for the journey it was decided that only one basket was usable so two more had to be purchased:

ii great Basketts and packing corde   iis xd (2s. 10d.)

The fishmonger was Mr. Gardiner, a merchant of standing, as the use of 'Mr.' (below) shows. He was presumably the James Gardiner who in the time of James I was one of the six wardens of The Mystery of the Fishmongers of the City of London.

Paid Mr. Gardiner for quarter of great owlde lings one
quarter of great new lings three quarters of newe
habardynes and Half a hundred of greene lings   xix li xiiis iijd (£9 13s. 2d.)

The cost of this order was nineteen pounds thirteen shillings and threepence. A haberdyne was a form of dried cod, the 'newe' meaning probably, unsalted. We do not speak of 'greene' fish any more, but to James Gardiner it meant 'fresh'. Gardiner was also able to supply salt for the preservation of his fish:

A quarter of white saulte   xiis (12s. 0d.)
to Porter for carrying salt to Mr. Gardiner   iiijd (4d.)
Paid porter for carrying downe of iii basketts from the Inne   iijd (3d.)
Given his man (a tip for loading)   xijd (12d.)

Gardiner's warehouse was in the Billingsgate district, so that Parker's homeward journey began by crossing London Bridge and paying toll of 4d. This probably means that his cart was 'shod', that is, it had bolts mounted in the wheels to give purchase if the cart became bogged down and it should be necessary for Parker to 'put his shoulder to the wheel'. The bolts, of course, helped to tear up the road surface and they accordingly paid toll at a higher rate. The final entry concerns the work of salting and preserving the catch:

Paid to Kennybie for ii days work at the Store howse doore and the
fishe chamber at xiiijd a day   iis iiijd (2s. 4d.)

About the same time, the household laid in its supplies of winter fuel. Twenty loads of billets (wood) and six loads of 'coles' were received between the 8th and 22nd of November and paid for at the rate of three shillings and threepence a load. The 'coles' were almost certainly charcoal for which Croydon was famous:

> The Collier that at Croydon doth dwell
> Men think he is cosin to the collier of Hell.

Names like Colliers Row and Colliers Wood remain to remind us of an industry which lasted well into the eighteenth century.

Sir Francis Carew was noted for his hospitality (it is referred to on his tomb) and there is evidence of this in the accounts. The weekly food bills (the later steward called them the 'Cates') which ran between £4 and £6 weekly rose to over £11 on the last week of December and to £13 on the first week of January, after which they reverted to the old level of spending. Extra crockery or plate needed was hired in London from Mr. Stapels who received twenty shillings, and, despite the effect of winter on the roads, Nicholas Parker made the double journey and was paid 'for carrying the vezell upp and Downe ijs. vjd.' and 'Wakemans wyfe' was paid sixpence for 'a day and a half to skower vezell'. The Christmas festivities meant extra work so 'Ester' was paid five shillings for 'helpinge the cooke in the Kitchen'; 'Burcotts wyfe' got eightpence for two days work; and even Widow New, who received a small payment during the year, a sort of pension, had eightpence for two days turning the spit.

Beer was homebrewed and its cost would be reckoned in the weekly 'cates', but the festive season also required six gallons of 'wyne' for which Mathew was paid twenty-four shillings. A luxury that was surely only for Sir Francis and his guests was: "Deliverid by your appoyntment to Noorhouse man for bringing a pownde granet orringes leamonds and a bottel of wine Vs." Sir Francis was fond of oranges as will afterwards appear. But Christmas is more than eating; there was music and dancing in the great hall; because way back in October Nick Swan was paid eightpence 'for bringing the base violl from Walton'; perhaps there was also a local variant of the mummer's play;

> Here come I old Father Christemas
> Welcome or welcome not,
> I hope old Father Christemas
> Will never be forgot.
> I have not come here for to laugh or to jeer
> But for a pocketful of money and a skinful of beer.

The New Year was the customary time for exchanging gifts, as appears from the tips given to those who brought them:

> Misteris Quarlis man for bringing anchoves   vj*d*.
> Nicholas Cokes mayde for bringing a pigg   vj*d*.
> Roger Lamberts sonne for bringing two fatt capons   vjd.

Sir Francis seems to have preferred to send money, at least to his young relatives. His nephew, Arthur Throckmorton, then a young gallant, noted in his diary a New Year gift from his uncle which he spent on silver lace, and tinsel, silver for his hat, a ring and tennis. The rest he lost at dice.

In addition to general supervision of his many estates, Sir Francis Carew was expected to play a full part in local government as a Justice of the Peace. Administration under the Tudors worked on the basis of local responsibilities, and the greater the possessions, the more was expected from the individual. From the peasant who turned out every year for his six days unpaid 'statute labour' upon the roads of his parish, up to the great landowner performing manifold duties as justice of the peace, the system was run at minimum cost to the central government. The hardest-worked of all unpaid officials were the justices. W. Lambarde, who wrote a handbook for their guidance, said that under Elizabeth, "so many not loads but stacks of statutes have been laid upon them."

The Justices, singly in the Petty Sessions or together at the Quarter Sessions, tried and sentenced wrongdoers for all except capital offences, and were completely responsible for law and public order within their own areas. Sir Francis Carew appointed the (unpaid) parish constable, and saw that he performed his duties. He rounded up and ordered the flogging of masterless men and sturdy beggars or issued 'licences to beg' to those whose misfortunes seemed to merit such a dispensation. He, and his fellows, inspected and licenced inns and innkeepers, issuing orders as required: "The said justices to discharge Ambrose Irons from keeping an alehouse in Carshalton Surrey, and to restrain him from keeping any other house of the same kind the said Ambrose Irons having encouraged certain trout stealers . . . and pursued other lewd courses." They controlled local wages and market prices.

As a magistrate he was also responsible for maintaining the roads, or at least for ordering some reluctant farmer to undertake the post (also unpaid) of Overseer of the Highways. Failure to carry out repairs could result in a reprimand from the Privy Council:

"An order to Lord Lumley and Sir Francis Carew to see that the Stretham end of Micham Lane is repaired as it is impassable to the detriment of the inhabitants of Beddington, Carshalton, Woodmansterne, Ewell (and one or two other places) causing both they and the Queen's messengers to go by other and inconvenient routes."

He was liable to receive orders from other bodies as well, as this from the Commissioners of Sewers in 1572:

"Francis Carew Esquer ... to cope and make higher than now is to ye quantity of one fote his banke against the river Biggre (Graveney) in the parish of Micham ... with goode faste and sounde earth as well for the keepinge in of the water as for the trampling of horsemen with treadinge it downe although it was latelye done."

His various duties included the despatch of prisoners to jails in Guildford or Southwark, the preparation of muster rolls of those eligible to serve in the county militia, and lists of those who failed to attend divine service. As patron of the churches in Beddington and at Walton on the Hill he appointed the Rectors and through them kept a general eye upon the morals of the parishes, particularly upon known harlots whose bastard children could become a charge on the community.

The Rector of St. Mary's was Sir Richard Worde, the 'Sir' being an honorary title, and he, in addition to the religious duties, collecting of tithes, and maintenance of the fabric and service books of his church, had a responsibility, under his patron, for the welfare services amongst his parishioners. He presided over the meeting in the vestry that elected churchwardens and overseers of the poor. The latter collected and distributed the poor rates for the relief of those in need. The church door was the official noticeboard for state proclamations and local orders which had to be read, and probably explained, to his congregations. He also read in church the appeals (called briefs) for good causes and disasters that came from time to time from his bishop, and made special collections for them. He entered in the Parish Registers details of christenings, marryings and buryings that had been a state requirement since 1538 (Beddington is one of the few parishes whose records go back to that date). He also undertook such education as was available to village children. He found time for other pleasures; the Registers record that his wife presented him with yet another offspring regularly every eighteen months. He finished with a total, equalling that of Nicholas Carew II, of seventeen children.

Sir Francis received frequent visits from his sister, Anne Throckmorton, and her young family. She hated France and the duties which kept her husband abroad, and spent much time suing for his release from foreign service. Her youngest daughter was born at Beddington and christened in St. Mary's with the name of Elizabeth on 16th April 1565. Bess Throckmorton—we will call her so as did most of her contemporaries—had such joyous memories of her childhood there, and probably of the indulgence of her bachelor uncle, that when the sad days came later in her life she dreamed of resting in the quiet churchyard. In 1571 her father died suddenly, perhaps of tuberculosis, possibly of overwork. Earnest and dedicated, his candid reports that never stooped to flattery, and his occasional indiscretions, were no way to wheedle favours out of the Queen though she respected his integrity and used his intelligence, not only in France, but later as a go-between in delicate missions with Mary Queen of Scots. Though

William Camden speaks of his 'small wealth', the list of his possessions sounds impressive enough. There were lands in Paulersbury (Northants) and manors at Alderminster and Sheriffs Lench, as well as a town house near St. Katherine Cree, but we will let Camden deliver his epitaph:

He was "a man of great experience, very ready wit and singular diligence who, busily attempting many things in Queen Mary's days, hardly saved his life by his eloquent wisdom; and under Queen Elizabeth having with indefatiguable pains discharged many embassies with great commendation, yet could he rise to but small wealth and those slight dignities (though glorious in title) of Chief Butler of England and Chamberlain of the Exchequer, whilst he showed himself an antagonist against Cecil in favour of Leicester. In whose house he was feeding hard at supper on salads when he was taken as some report with an Impostume of the lungs, as others say, with violent catarrh and died . . . in good time for himself and his, being in great danger of losing life and estate by his restless spirit."

Anne Throckmorton did not remain long a widow; perhaps with her seven children to bring up it was essential for her to remarry. She married Adrian Stokes, a childless widower, and with their joint possessions they lived a life of comfortable affluence. Of her children, only two, Bess and Nicholas, aged six and nine respectively when their father died, continued to have close ties with their uncle and with Beddington. Arthur Throckmorton inherited eventually his father's estates and with them became the head of the family, living a full life as courtier, soldier, and country gentleman. Apart from the occasional receipt of new-year gifts from Sir Francis Carew he maintained little contact. The other four children fade completely from the picture. Anne died in 1587 and is buried with her first husband in St. Botolph's Church, Aldersgate.

On Sunday 8th November, 1584 Bess was taken by her brother Arthur to Hampton Court to be interviewed by the Vice Chamberlain and sworn of the Privy Chamber as Maid of Honour to the Queen. She was nearly twenty, tall, of medium colouring, with blue eyes, and, if she was hardly a beauty, she had a sparkle that came of her father's proud and independent spirit. Her education, one guesses, was not good, her letters are grammatically poor, and even for an age when one customarily spelt as one wished, her spelling was unusual. Nit (as she spelt it in a famous letter to her brother quoted later) is but a poor attempt at Night.

She was of an age when she might hope for marriage, but Elizabethan marriages were seldom for love and much more often for the substantial portion which the bride could bring to her husband. Bess could bring but little, even the sum of £500 which she had been left by her father was lent to the Earl of Huntingdon and though throughout her life she endeavoured to regain it from the Earl and his heirs it was never repaid. Her court appointment, the result of some months of letters and interviews on the part of her brother, gave her an assured position, with perhaps the hope that the Queen might at some time graciously help her to a husband.

In the summer of 1587 England talked of war. In London the citizens who had greeted the news of the execution of Mary Queen of Scots with the pealing of joybells and bonfires in the streets, now marched and drilled with pike and musket in the knowledge that if the Duke of Parma were not repelled their city might suffer the carnage that had destroyed Antwerp. The countryside was less well organised. Local defence was the responsibility of the Lord Lieutenant of the County; in the case of Surrey, of Lord Howard of Effingham. He was responsible for raising the county militia and he relied upon the Justices of the Peace to aid him. It was for a moment such as this that Sir Francis Carew and his fellow justices had discouraged such unlawful (because unwarlike) games as football and throwing of the stone and had done their best to foster military skills like shooting with the longbow. The longbow promised to be a poor weapon against Parma's veteran professional army. Not for the last time England rushed into a war for which she was totally unprepared.

The hundred yeomen who attended the Queen were our only permanent soldiers. The trained bands of London were the best equipped of our citizen soldiers, but even they had experienced no actual alarm since Wyatt's rebellion thirty years before; their battle experience since was limited to the occasional apprentice riot. Sir Francis had already played a significant part in the militia, being nominated in 1584 as one of the four captains to command the 1,000 men raised and equipped by the county. Their enthusiasm had so pleased the queen that she promised after seeing "how forward the gentlemen were and the goodwill of the people" that "they shall be imployed only for the garde of our person." The following year she ordered "understanding that . . . there are great stoare of stout vagabonds and maysterless men able inoughe for labour, which do great hurt in the county by their idle and naughtie life" the strongest and most able of them were to be sent to the Port of London for transportation to the Low Countries "where they shall be well used and entertained".

Howard had far more pressing obligations as commander of the fleet, so on 23rd July 1587 he enrolled four deputy lieutenants, Sir William More of Loseley, Sir Francis Carew, Sir Thomas Browne, and William Howard, to cope with mustering and equipping the extra men now demanded by the Privy Council. The Council asked originally for another 4,000 men from Surrey, but it was later abated to 2,000 of whom 400 of the strongest and squarest of men 'were to bear arquebuses, 600 were to carry bows, another 600 were to be armed with bills, and 400 equipped with corselets and pikes'. The next duty was to seek out all those who "most obstinantlie have refused to come to church to praiers and divine service" to surprise and unfurnish them of their armour, leaving only such weapons as might be necessary for them to defend their houses. If the Spaniards should land they were for their own protection to be committed to prison. The deputies were commanded to counteract all rumours with which, in the absence of official news, the country was rife, and to establish and man a chain of beacon points throughout the county. Sir Francis had a special responsibility for Tumble Beacon in Banstead; it was particularly important as its light could be seen from the City. No one knew just where the Spaniards might be expected to land, and England could little afford to keep the nation waiting under arms; so the men of the militia were to hold themselves in readiness and only assemble when the beacons flared and a Spanish landing was imminent. On 10th August, in the middle of their preparations, a false alarm was circulated that 120 sail, supposed Spaniards, had been seen off the coast of the West Country, and the deputies were ordered to "put in order of defence with as little noise and hindrance of harvest as may be".

On July 23rd 1588, with the Spanish Armada actually under way off the Isle of Wight, the instructions still suggest a woeful lack of organisation. The Deputies were "to be in readyness upon the flering of . . . becons to resort to oppose soche attempt as the enemy may make to sett on lande his forces in any place". They were to avoid confusion and ensure "that no other persons be suffered to assemble together beside the ordinary bands . . . to set watches in every thoroughfare and town to stay and apprehend all vagabonds, rogues and other suspected persons and if they be found with any manifest offence tending to stir trouble or rebellion to cause such to be executed by martial law." At last the levies were to be raised and equipped, and eight Lances and ninety light horse were to be despatched to Brentwood by 27th July; and a thousand footmen were ordered to "Stratford on the Bow" by the 29th. In fact, assuming that the Surrey forces arrived in time, the decisive battle was at that moment being fought off Gravelines.

At the time it was only slowly realised that the Armada was defeated and the danger was over. Preparations continued with the main camp at Tilbury. We do not know whether Sir Francis was with his men, or whether his duties kept him at home arresting dubious rogues and vagabonds. One guesses that he was present four months later at the thanksgiving in St. Paul's Cathedral, when "the Queen attended by the nobility, judges, heralds and trumpeters, all on horseback, came in a chariot supported by four pillars and drawn by two white horses to St. Paul's Church, where alighting at the West Door, she fell on her knees and audibly praised God for her own and the Nation's signal deliverance."

The scattering of the Armada did not end the work of the Deputies. The war continued, and a state or readiness had to be maintained. Muster rolls were prepared; levies trained and equipped for retaliatory actions on the Spanish coast. In 1593, Lord Howard circulated a rebuke to all his deputies "touching the high charge of £100 for the coats, hose, stockings, shirts, shoes and swords of the fifty soldiers levied in the shire of Surrey for service in the Low Countries with Sir Francis de Vere". Two pounds a head hardly seems excessive! But then two pounds was the annual income of Mrs. Housekeeper Tegge. The flow of circulars to the deputies continued; there were more queries about equipment supplied; another ordered that the excessive cost of grain should be reduced. A report was called for on the Jesuits in Surrey and a personal rebuke came for Sir Thomas Browne who was urged "to give more time and pains to being a deputy lieutenant".

A country gentleman certainly had to give time and pains!

CHAPTER SEVEN

Bess Throckmorton and Sir Walter Ralegh

DURING THESE eventful years, Elizabeth Throckmorton remained maid-of-honour to the Queen; and if it was her hope that her position might help her to find a husband, there seemed small chance of its fulfilment. Her duties brought her into daily contact with the most glittering figure of a Court where fine clothes and magnificent presence were a requirement for men as well as women. Sir Walter Ralegh was Captain of the Queen's Guard. His silver armour, the jewels upon his person and the hilt of his sword, his dark hair and ivory complexion, his light sweet voice and beauty, made a combination that no woman could resist, and few men entirely trust. It is not within the scope of this book to attempt to form an estimate of this controversial and enigmatic character. Was he romantic hero, or ruthless adventurer, selfish and damnably proud, or just a typical man of his age? To Londoners, who hated him, he was "that great Lucifer" but to the sailors of his native west country, who loved him, he was their hero and the only man who could control them. To the Parliament men of a generation later he was an outspoken critic of Royal supremacy. Biographers differ today.

It is obvious that such a man, continually about the court, could, and did, sway the hearts of any of the maids-of-honour whom he chose to notice. John Aubrey, with his love of scandal, reports in his quaint way:

> He loved a wench well, and one time getting up one of the Maids of Honour up against a tree in a wood ('twas his first lady), who seemed at first boarding to be something fearful of her honour and modest, she cried, "Sweet Sir Walter, what do you me ask? Will you undo me? Nay Sweet Sir Walter. Sweet Sir Walter. Sir Walter." At last as the danger and the pleasure at the same time grew higher, she cried in ecstasy, "Swisser Swatter, Swisser Swatter."

The lady is thought not to be our Bess, who served the queen for seven years before she too fell victim to his charms.

As in everything Ralegh did, it is impossible to discover his true feelings. In his posthumously published "Instructions to his Son" he advises "have therefore ever more care that thou be beloved of thy wife rather than thyself besotted on her." Yet, under the name of 'Serena' he addressed to Bess a charmingly mannered love lyric

> Nature that washed her hands in milk
> And had forgot to dry them,
> Instead of earth took snow and silk
> At Loves request to try them,
> If she a mistress could compose
> To please Love's fancy out of those.

18. *Believed to be Lady Ralegh, this engraving is taken from a painting hanging in the National Gallery, Dublin*

Her eyes he would should be of light,
A violet breath and lips of jelly,
Her hair not black nor overbright,
And of the softest down her belly;
As for her inside he'd have it
Only of wantonness and wit.

He did not however, as others have done, deny the deed. They were secretly married in November 1592, and the gossip was passed around the Court, without reaching for some time, it seems, the ears of the Queen. During the last stages of her pregnancy Bess withdrew to her brother Arthur's protection in a house in the Mile End Road while Ralegh worked frantically upon the Queen to obtain permission for a privateering voyage that would place him safely upon the high seas when the scandal broke. He was almost successful. The child was born on 29th March and christened in the presence of the Earl of Essex (strange choice in view of the deadly rivalry between the two men), and sent with a nurse to Enfield. A month later, Bess returned to her duties with the Queen while Ralegh sped to Falmouth to embark on his ship. The child must have died in infancy; even its existence was unknown, and frequently denied by Ralegh's biographers, until Dr. Rowse discovered the diary of Arthur Throckmorton.

There were too many enemies of Ralegh at Court for the deception to last for ever. The Queen's anger was intense. The lovers were committed to separate cells in the Tower, from which Ralegh was released after five weeks, and Bess six months later. Despite all his arts of flattery he never completely regained the trust of his sovereign; though he retained his post of Captain of the Guard, along with the estates at Sherborne and the use of Durham House (on the site of Charing Cross Station) as a town mansion. Bess, she neither forgave nor saw again. Perhaps Bess did not care. She had succeeded against all odds in marrying the most dazzling man in the country, and if the marriage was to bring further imprisonment, separation, and tragedy, and if she could never enter fully into her husband's intellectual life, her love never faltered, and Ralegh, looking back upon the ten years that followed, could say "I chose you and I loved you in my happiest times".

The marriage of his niece brought Sir Francis Carew into contact with the great Elizabethan. They may already have been acquainted, as both of them owned property in Mitcham, where a water mill near Mitcham bridge was long pointed out, perhaps with justification, as Ralegh's snuff mill. The other property, a house in Mitcham which stood on the corner of Whitford Lane and was sold to pay the expenses of Ralegh's second Guiana expedition, is described as part of Bess's marriage portion, though how she acquired it, unless it was a gift from her uncle, is unclear. The colonising voyages which Ralegh promoted brought back a number of plants which might be commercially useful, and with which Sir Francis is reputed to have experimented in his kitchen garden. Apart from tobacco, the most important introduction was the potato, for which there is a long-standing tradition that it was first grown in Beddington. Lilac is another plant attributed to Ralegh, but when the Earl of Dorset wrote to Sir Francis asking for specimen plants it was for asparagus, myrtle and orange trees that he asked. Oranges were Carew's great success. The trees grown from seed were planted on the south facing side of a great wall constructed in his grounds and so shielded from the worst of the weather. The trees had further protection from frosts by what John Evelyn called "a tabernacle of boards" which

19. The Orangery wall, Beddington

may well have been a tent-like structure with canvas screens and heating stoves placed amongst them. The operation could well have been seen by Sir Francis while on his travels in Italy, or planned for him by an expatriate Italian, since similar structures can still be seen around Naples. Local patriotism likes to associate Ralegh with everything, but to claim, as Bentham does, that the seed was brought by him from Florida is absurd. That there was a connection between the two men is almost certain; but the orange pips are far more likely to have travelled in the opposite direction across the Atlantic.

Despite the proximity of Croydon and Nonsuch Palaces, both much used by the Queen on her annual progresses, Sir Francis had to wait many years for the expensive honour of a visit from Elizabeth. It was not until 17th August 1599 that she came from Nonsuch for a three day stay. What it cost him in cash and provisions is not known. His neighbour, Sir Julius Caesar of Mitcham, boasted, or should it be complained, that a one night visit cost him £700 sterling "besides my own provision and what was sent in by my friends". Like children at a party, it was the custom to reward the Queen with expensive presents before she departed. Sir Julius gave her a gown, a taffeta hat, and a jewel of gold set with diamonds and rubies, but Sir Francis had a novelty of a different order. Using, perhaps, the same screens that protected his orange plants, he erected a dampened tent over his cherry tree, and so delayed the ripening of the fruit for a full month. He was thereby able to present the Queen with a dish of her favourite fruit a month after all the other trees in England had ceased to bear. Her three days' stay probably cleared the whole crop. There can be little doubt that her second visit, almost to the day twelve months later, was to see whether he could repeat the trick.

The famous orange trees receive no mention at this stage, presumably because they were not yet large enough to bear fruit. For more than a century they flourished and became one of the curiosities of England. John Evelyn, Daniel Defoe, John Aubrey and many other less well known tourists came to see them; it was the only place in the country where they could see orange trees growing in open ground. The wall rebuilt in the eighteenth century to accommodate trees now grown to thirteen feet high and the "tabernacle of boards and stoves" were the subject of many glowing descriptions. They produced, as the gardeners told John Gibson, 10,000 fruit in a season. Like all Carew activities this was no dilettante operation but full scale commercial production. The famous orangery also set a fashion in large and small houses from Kensington Palace downwards for an orangery to be provided, but these were mere conservatory rooms where trees could be cultivated in tubs; nowhere else was the Carew experiment repeated.

The trees lasted until the bitter winter of 1739-40 when the Thames froze so hard that an ice-fair was held upon it. In the bitter weather the stoves placed amongst the trees failed, or were insufficient, and the trees died. A huge red brick wall nearly 200 feet long remains. It is a plain wall and is not "Honeycombed with flues and pipes" as Bentham could have seen if he had examined it.

Not far from Carew Manor* is a grove of trees still called Queen Elizabeth's Walk; there is no reason to doubt the village tradition that the ageing Queen used the pleasant

---

* The term 'Carew Manor' will henceforward be used in its modern sense to mean the Mansion House of the Carews. This has in fact had several names in the past, West Court, Beddington Place and Beddington Park House are some of them. The present title has only been used since 1954.

20. *A portrait of Queen Elizabeth 1st by an unknown artist c. 1575*

path for gentle exercise. At least until the 1830s, "Ladye Walk", as it was then called, was a place of promenade for village gentlefolk.

No contemporary plan remains of the gardens as laid out by Sir Francis, but Thomas Fuller said that "by virtue of the waters they are a paradise of pleasure". He was perhaps remembering the book of Genesis, "and the river went out of Eden to water the garden and from thence it was parted and became four heads". The fourfold plot, divided by canals, was an oriental feature freely adopted by the Elizabethans in their formal gardens, and the eighteenth century layout would lend itself well to this plan.

The device was advised by Francis Bacon in his essay 'On Gardens' ". . . the garden is best to be square encompassed on all four sides by a stately arched hedge"; above the arches little turrets were to be set large enough to hold a cage of birds "and over the space between the arches some other little figure with broad plates of round coloured glass gilt for the sun to play upon". Whether the Beddington gardens went so far is not known, but one feature that Bacon recommended certainly did exist.

> I wish in the middle a fair mount with three ascents and alleys enough for four to walk abreast which I would have a perfect circle without any bulwarks or embellishments; and the whole mount to be thirty feet high surmounted by a fine banqueting house with some chimneys neatly cast.

There are accounts from 1650 of repairs to the little house by the mount and to the mount house. The little house may have been the summerhouse shown in Bentham's book, but the pavilion upon the mount was decorated by a painting of the Armada and contained a red and white marble table that Aubrey says Sir Francis brought home from his travels abroad (this, incidentally, is the only reference to him as a traveller). If the mount was not levelled by later owners, it must have been at the far end of the garden just beyond the present fence where a considerable bank still exists; a pleasant situation for a pavilion, because the river formerly made a considerable cascade here.

While Sir Francis tended his kitchen garden, his distant cousins in the west country were bringing still greater fame to the name of Carew. Sir Peter Carew, who belonged to the main branch of the family still living at Mohuns Ottery, joined the service of Henry VIII soon after the execution of Sir Nicholas, and his life of adventure deserves a fuller biography than is appropriate here. In his youth he had served as a professional soldier in Italy and the Netherlands. He was knighted by Henry VIII, but as an opponent of Mary's marriage to Philip II, and kinsman of Edward Courtenay, he fled the country after Wyatt's rebellion. Traced to Antwerp, he was brought back to the Tower for the rest of the reign. Released by Elizabeth, his restless spirit led him to Ireland in an attempt to regain the Barony and estates of Idrone. He was soon in trouble for engaging in the civil war there; but he achieved his objective, and died in 1575 as Constable of that same Tower in which he had once been held as a prisoner. He prepared a very detailed will showing the many branches of his family and the order of seniority amongst them. He left no children, and the ancestral home of Mohuns Ottery passed to his sister while the newly won barony was willed to pass to his cousin Peter, and after him to George Carew (which it actually did) and if they died without heirs it was to go to the Carews of Bickleigh and if they failed, to the Carews of Haccombe. If they should become extinct it should pass to the Carews of Antony and if they too should die out, to "Sir Nicholas Carew of Benyngton [sic] in Surrey" and finally to Carew of Edmonsbury. His cousin George, who had helped in the Irish adventure, lived as full a life as soldier,

21, 22. *ABOVE LEFT Queen Elizabeth's Walk. This section still exists between Queenswood Avenue and Croydon Road, Wallington RIGHT. The kitchen garden wall, Carew Manor*

statesman and family historian, and was created Earl of Totnes by James I. In Antony, a stay-at-home Carew named Richard achieved a longer-lasting fame as the writer of "A Survey of Cornwall" published in 1602.

A frequent visitor to Beddington was young Nicholas Throckmorton whose hopes must have risen higher as his uncle approached his sixties and remained unmarried. Very little is known of his early life. During his father's lifetime, he and his brothers were brought up by a tutor, Francis Goldsmith. As the fifth son, he, brother Henry, and sister Elizabeth received £500 apiece under his father's will. When his mother died at her home near St. Katherine Cree he received "a hanging bed with its bedding, some gilt jugs and a jewel", while Bess, still undisgraced and in the service of the Queen, was to have all her jewels, chains, wearing apparel and linen. Sir Francis Carew was also remembered, receiving a gilt bowl with a cover and a striking clock to stand upon a cupboard.

The following year—it was 1588—he spent in Italy; and brother Arthur sent him an allowance through a banker in Lucca. Italy was a strange place for a young man of twenty-six during England's hour of peril. He was possibly aware of Sir Philip Sidney's instructions "your purposes being a gentleman, to furnish yourself with the knowledge of all such things as may be serviceable to your country." He spent some years travelling, for the Phillipps collection has a certificate of his matriculation at the University of Padua in 1590. He was back in England later in the year, and able to lend £300 to Arthur who was rebuilding the family mansion at Paulersbury. The loan was repaid in instalments along with the annuity of £40 that his brother allowed him.

In 1591 he came to Beddington with an alarming rumour. Ralegh and Essex were leading a joint expedition against the city of Cadiz. Arthur Throckmorton had joined the force, and London was buzzing with the news that the raid had been a total failure and Ralegh drowned. The fears were needless; Arthur returned safely with a knighthood, one of many distributed by Essex.

About this time Nicholas married Mary, the eldest daughter of Sir William More of Loseley, the fellow Deputy Lieutenant of Sir Francis. His expectations of fortune were good enough to make him acceptable to his father-in-law; unlike John Donne who was rash enough to elope with seventeen-year-old Anne, the younger daughter. The poet was dragged through the law courts and all but ruined by the irascible Sir William. Donne took refuge, in "poverty and illness", in Mitcham, whence he composed a letter full of self-pity; writing, he said, "from my hospital at Mitcham where there is not one person beside myself well . . . I flatter myself that I am dying too".

There may have been times when Sir William had doubts about the favoured son-in-law who experienced continuous financial crises, and wrote to him in 1604 saying "my plate is all in pawn, credit have I none . . . you know whereon I do hope and to whom I am indebted which may frustrate my hopes if I should not content and please . . . No less than £200 at Midsummer next can make me show my face in any company, and £100 at Michelmas next which if I cannot have I must leave my country, and my wife and children to the parish." Even more worrying for Nicholas was the fact that he was not alone in the field. Sir Francis had other sisters and other nephews. Mary, the wife of Sir Arthur Darcy had two sons; Arthur, who was eventually to inherit Sutton and Epsom and to squander both away rapidly, and Francis in whose company and conversation the ageing uncle took great delight.

The necessity of fawning in order to content and please was not something that came easily to a Throckmorton. But if Nicholas had problems, his sister was entering the blackest period of her life.

The great hall of Beddington was the scene of a further act in the tragedy of Ralegh. Queen Elizabeth died at Richmond Palace on March 24th 1603, and while the heralds were proclaiming her death at the gates of Whitehall Palace messengers were speeding north to inform King James of Scotland that his inheritance was come at last. James was not taken unaware by the news. He had been kept informed stage by stage in a secret correspondence with Robert Cecil. Each of the other great ones around the dying queen had endeavoured also to carry on a communication which was technically treasonable. In the scramble each courtier believed that one of the easiest ways of ingratiating himslf with the new monarch was by denigrating the others.

Ralegh was late in making his approaches. By the time his overtures arrived, James had received plenty of warnings about "Bloody Ralegh and his damnable pride". James, moreover, by temperament and policy saw himself as a peacemaker who could bring to an end the tip-and-run raiding and the privateering voyages into which the war had degenerated. Ralegh therefore had a chilling reception. "Thou art Ralegh and rawly have I heard of you."

Plague raged in London during the summer of 1603 and our most timorous of monarchs spent much time circling his capital. This probably explains how it was that Ralegh met the king at Beddington. He had already been dismissed his post as Captain of the Guard and his place given to Sir Thomas Erskine, a Scot. His pride forced him to believe that he could restore himself to favour by a bold stroke that would bring victory to English arms and profit to the new king. Patiently, with the candlelight flickering upon the great hammer beams, he presented the plan outlined in his "Discourse concerning a War with Spain". In 1595 he had sailed to the mouth of the Orinoco River where he learned how the natives hated and feared the Spaniards. They had listened with awe to his tales of a Great White Queen, a virgin who lived beyond the seas and who could save them from the Spaniards if they would but join with her. In return they told him of the land of gold far in the interior. Both sides were spinning a yarn to please the other, but Ralegh's sanguine temperament had been captivated by the idea of South American gold.

He must have reminded the king of his voyage; and would be willing, he said, to raise at his own expense, and lead, 2,000 men from his beloved west country. A bold stroke could sever the West Indies from Spanish rule and give the English ships a secure base from which to intercept the treasure ships of Spain, and from that base he would lead the quest for fabled Eldorado. He no doubt revived arguments that he had used to the Queen in 1595: send to Guiana not soldiers, but experts and military advisers, build up the Inca forces to fight for themselves against Spanish oppression, bring back the natural leaders to England, educate them in Christianity, train, and, if necessary, marry them to English women before sending them back to become the masters of a great new Indian state. The charge to the Crown would be minimal, the rewards in tribute and trade fantastic.

The proposition had failed to impress Elizabeth's frugal but practical mind and to James every word was confirmation of his belief that here was a dangerous and overmighty subject whose powers must be curtailed without delay.

The answer to the Beddington proposals came rapidly. Ralegh was given a fortnight to vacate Durham House, and he must relinquish the Lordship of the Stannaries. A month later he was in Winchester awaiting trial on a charge of High Treason. The

Londoners had howled and jeered as he was removed from the Tower en route for Winchester.

Of the trial, a travesty of justice, and subsequent sentence of death; of the twelve years he endured as a prisoner in the Tower with his sentence suspended but never reprieved, it is not necessary to detail here. Much of the time Bess became a voluntary captive with him, and it was during his imprisonment that his second son, Carew Ralegh, was born in 1605. During those years the future can never have seemed so insecure to the youngest children of Sir Nicholas Throckmorton.

The new reign brought threats of disaster to many others in the district whose livelihood or pleasure was derived from the river Wandle. William Heliar, King's Chaplain and Archdeacon of Barnstable put forward a plan to tap the Wandle waters between Croydon and Waddon and convey them by undergound pipes to supply the rapidly expanding city of London. He proposed to use the profits of the undertaking to found, in the name of the king, a College of Divinity at Chelsea. The prospect of losing even one tenth of their waters produced such a howl of protest from the farmers, mealmen, millers, bakers, Thames boatmen, and country gentlemen, that the king was forced to appoint a commission to enquire into the scheme. The Commission was hardly an impartial body. It was headed by the Archbishop of Canterbury and the Earl of Nottingham (the latter, once Lord Howard of Effingham, now resident in Haling Park) as well as Sir Francis Carew, and it included most of the other landowners in the district.

Predictably the report was strongly against the project. The river along its nine mile course between Waddon and Wandsworth was turning the water wheels of no less then twenty-four corn mills as well as other industries on its banks, and, in years of drought at least, the waters were insufficient for the task. Many mills, they said, were forced to remain idle for up to twelve hours out of the twenty-four while the water was penned up to provide a working head. They continued "And it hath been likewise proved unto us that divers poore men dwelling about two or three miles from Beddington, Waddon and Carshalton, whereas there be six mills upon the said river . . . having brought upon their neckes a bushell of corne . . . have gone from mill to mill . . . and could not have their corne ground for want of water." They went on to report that the springs above Waddon were known in times of drought to have dried up so that the "Trowtes therein being have dyed for want of fresh water" while the inhabitants were forced to dig ditches to retain enough water for their cattle. Further, the scheme would do damage to the Archbishop's Palace, to the Earl of Exeter whose mansion was at Wimbledon, and to Sir Francis Carew "in respect of the force wch he hath upon the saide river wch conveyeth water to the house . . . and in regard of the greate costes bestowed upon the said River for the delight of our late Soveraigne Lady the Queenes Majestie and continued for the pleasure of the Kinges most . . . Majesty." The effects would be felt, they claimed, in Kingston, Croydon, Reigate, and Dorking whose markets supplied the corn ground in the area, as well as in Brentwood, and in the City of London itself. The Report was delivered on 26th November 1610 and in the face of such determined opposition the scheme was abandoned. The Wandle waters were safe for another 250 years.

CHAPTER EIGHT

Sir Nicholas Throckmorton Carew

S IR FRANCIS CAREW died on 16th May 1611 at the age of 81. His death brought an end to the immediate financial embarrassments of Nicholas Throckmorton, who inherited the name and arms of Carew, along with the bulk of the estates, except for Sutton and Epsom which went to the elder Darcy cousin, and Walton on the Hill which Sir Francis left to Francis Darcy, and desired Nicholas not to contest the grant.

Nicholas provided "his deare and well deserving unckle" with a splendid tomb in the family chapel. The life-sized statue of Sir Francis, dressed in full armour, but wearing the skull cap commonly assumed by elderly Elizabethans, lies upon an altar tomb of sculptured alabaster. Two columns of black marble support an enriched entablature which encloses shields with the arms of his many ancestors, and two marble panels proclaim his virtues in Latin and his career in English. On the front of the tomb, in low relief, are the kneeling figures of Nicholas, bareheaded and in armour, and Mary, his wife, wearing a ruff and long cloak. Behind them are the smaller figures of his five sons and two daughters.

For Nicholas the wealth unbounded that had filled his hopes and dreams for so many years had as many vexations as his life of poverty. As a new landlord he may have experienced some of the troubles of Abraham Cowley at Chertsey, who wrote, "I can get no money from my tenants and have my meadows eaten up every night by cattle put in by my neighbours". The provision of a suitable monument, the settlement of his own pressing debts and of those left by Sir Francis, left little ready cash to pay the many legacies in his uncle's will. It was not until 1623 that the £100 bequeathed to the poor of Beddington, and the similar sum to Walton, could be paid off, although the Overseers of the Poor in the two parishes received annual payments of £7 each by way of interest. The £100 due to Thomasin Worde, ninth daughter of Sir Francis's many-progenied rector was paid in the same year but without interest. It seems less than generous to a girl who signed her elaborate quit-claim with a cross twelve years after the money was bequeathed. After years of genteel poverty, Mary Carew did not live long to enjoy her new position, but no memorial marks her grave; Nicholas married again, to a widow, Susan Bright. They were married in St. Mary Woolnoth on 14th August 1616, and the Brights, a London family, were delighted to discover that their daughter was now sister-in-law to Sir Walter Ralegh. She died in 1633 having added a daughter and a son to Nicholas's already large family. A tablet, now lost, was placed in the chapel by her son, Thomas; it was dedicated "to the memory of my deare mother the Lady Carew ... whose virtuous life doth Memory preserve who taught her children Heaven's great God to serve." More impressive, if less sincere, is the lead tablet erected in the same year to his steward Thomas Greenhill, which was placed in the church by William Greenhill, his brother and Mary, his sister;

Under thy feete, interred is here,
A native born in Oxfordsheer;
First Life and Learning Oxford gave,
Surrey him his death and grave.
He once a Hill was fresh and Green,
Now withered is not to be seen;
Earth in Earth shoueld up is shut,
A Hill into a Hole is put;
That Darksome earth by Power Divine,
Bright at last as Sun may shine.

If one detects in Nicholas some parsimony in one who had endured poverty for much of his life, one wonders what was his response to the barefaced cheek of a begging letter from the Earl of Holderness:

Sir Nicholas Carew, I have not yett soe much acquayntance with you as to intreate a bucke from you, but if it should please you to pleasure me with one to the bearer hereof I shall be redie to requite your kindness whensoever you shall have occasion to use me for the like in a greter matter, and rest your very lovinge freind. Holdernes.

Begging letters may be ignored, though, as the Earl was the new Lieutenant of the County, he probably got his buck; but a great landowner was liable to face other trials. A friend wrote to warn him that Sir Francis Stydolf and a hundred and fifty others planned to descend on Beddington House in "a great conspiracy not against your person, but against your vittayles."

History is full of stories where the beginnings are unknown and the endings forgotten. The Laing papers have a curiously involved report dated May 18th 1623 which is given in full for the sake of its local colour and also for the pronunciation, at least amongst the lower orders, of the name Carew. A Spanish messenger carrying letters to the King was robbed near Dartford of more than £100 in Spanish gold pieces, and an agent named Francis Hawkins was sent to comb the taverns of Dartford to look for a man dressed in canvas seaman's clothes who had Spanish gold about him. Hawkins' report which was made at the request of Sir John Tonstall of Addiscombe tells that eventually he fell in with a man named Cowrtoppe who said he was to go "to Sir Nicholas Cary with a letter which he had brought from beyond the sea, saying he had landed at Brighthelmstone upon Tuesday last." Hawkins told him that he was going that way for he must go to his mother who dwelt at Croydon and Cowrtoppe told him "if he would go in his company thither he would give him his dinner there." This they did, Hawkins noticing that he had Spanish gold and also "a big purse fastened between his drawers and the under breeches full of money"; as they travelled they talked and Cowrtoppe told him that "he knew one George Hawkins well, an alehouse keeper at Banstead and also Sir Nicholas Cary's cook whose name I have forgotten (but he was brought up as a boy under Sir Francis Cary) and said he would see him." They parted at last but when Hawkins saw that his companion was going towards Mitcham "he told him that that was not the way to Beddington and he answered he would go along by the park pale and if he did meet with the keeper that would serve his turn." So Cowrtoppe walks off with his purse full of Spanish gold towards Mitcham and into oblivion.

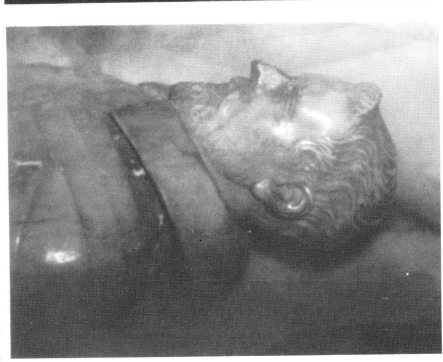

23, 24. *Sir Francis Carew (left) and Sir Nicholas Throckmorton Carew (right) from effigies in St. Mary's Church; the effigy of Sir Francis is recumbent*

Confusion between Carys and Carews frequently happens not only to the consternation of the historian. Even contemporaries were sometimes unclear about who was which. There is an anecdote of Queen Elizabeth who, having had the difference of spelling and pronunciation explained to her, by two members of the families, summed it up by saying, "You are Cary and what care you and you are Carew and what care I."

Nicholas Throckmorton Carew was knighted in January 1613 and appointed Chamberlain of the Exchequer, a post that had been held by his father. Of his activities in this employment nothing is known. Residence in Beddington would not have been incompatible with working at court, but the Carews always seem to have had houses in London at their disposal. It is possible that the house in Broad Street, later much used by his sister, Elizabeth, was his property, or that he was using another in the parish of St. Katherine Cree that had belonged to his brother Thomas. His niece, Anne Throckmorton, petitioned the Archbishop of Canterbury in April 1612, claiming that her uncle Thomas had left the house to her but that "the said Nicholas Throckmorton now called by the name of Nicholas Carew Knight... do go about to defeat your suppliant".

Nicholas also served as a knight of the shire in the Parliament of 1621 and from 1623 onwards as deputy Lieutenant of the county.

Some time during the morning of 29th October 1618 a rider clattered with all speed between Westminster and Beddington. His arrival was perhaps not unexpected; he bore a distraught note for Sir Nicholas from his sister. It read:–

> My best brother, Sir Nicholas Carew, at Beddington.
> I desiar, good brother, that you will be pleased to let my berri the worthi boddi of my nobell husband Sir Walter Ralegh in your church at beddington wher I desiar to be berred. The lords have given me his ded boddi, though they denied me his life. This nit hee shall be brought you with two or three of my men.
> Let me he'r presently,
> God hold me in my wites.
> E.R.

For Ralegh the end of the tragedy had been reached. He had endured twelve years of imprisonment in the Tower, helped no doubt in his ordeal by the presence with him of Elizabeth in voluntary captivity. Then, briefly, freedom while he voyaged to Guiana to seek the gold of which he had at last persuaded the king he held the secret. But whatever the excitement of feeling once more the fresh sea air upon his cheeks, and however sanguine his gambler's hope, he must have known in his heart that the voyage was so hedged by conditions imposed by that faint-hearted monarch, that it could never succeed.

He had returned old, broken, and sick, his expedition a total failure, his son Wat dead in the fighting with Spanish forces, to a king who had even before the start refused to lift the sentence of death under which he had endured since 1603. When his ship, the *Destiny*, had docked at Plymouth it was met by Sir Lewis Stukeley, Vice Admiral of Devon, and his grieving wife. The former was charged to convey him once more into captivity.

There had been no further trial. The fickle Londoners who had howled for his blood in 1603 recognised him now for what he was, the last of the great Elizabethan adventurers, and would have made vocal their support at any public hearing.

From the Tower, from which even Bess was now excluded, he had been taken by boat to Westminster for examination, where he learned that the fifteen-year-old sentence

25. Sir Walter Ralegh and one of his sons from a portrait by an unknown artist

was to be carried out on the following morning. Bess came late that night to where he was lodged in the gate tower of Westminster Abbey. She had been under house arrest during the last days lest she should make a dash abroad with her jewels which might be confiscated by Ralegh's creditors. She was able to tell him that the only result of all her letters and petitions was a promise that she should have the disposal of his body. No doubt she assured him that he would rest at Beddington. She left at midnight and perhaps scribbled and despatched the note to her brother during the small hours.

Early in the morning of the 29th, Ralegh, carefully dressed in black velvet, was led into Old Palace Yard to die. Only the bulk of Henry VII's chapel and St. Margaret's Church remain unchanged. The buildings that linked St. Margaret's with the rambling old Palace of Westminster have been swept away, and the Palace itself, burned in the fire of 1834, replaced by the present Houses of Parliament. In the centre of the enclosed court the scaffold had been erected. Now that death was certain, Ralegh faced it with a dignity and courage that he had not always shown during the long years of adversity.

I have many sins for which to beseech God's pardon. Of a long time my course was a course of vanity. I have been a seafaring man, a soldier, and a courtier, and in the temptations of the least of these there is enough to overthrow a good mind, and a good man.

The axe fell twice and the head was severed.

Lady Ralegh probably witnessed the gruesome ceremony from a coach drawn up near the buildings. The bleeding head, having been exhibited to the crowd, was placed in a red leather bag and wrapped in Ralegh's velvet cloak. The bundle was then handed into the mourning coach which drove off while the headless corpse was carried into St. Margaret's. Inside, in the register of burials, the parish clerk wrote:

Sir Walter Rawleigh Knight October 1618.

No recent biographer has speculated upon what happened next. A. L. Rowse assumes that the woman who had dared the wrath of a queen, bombarded the king and Lords with letters, petitions and personal appeals for clemency, and who was to spend much of the rest of her life in litigation over details of her husband's estates was content to receive less than she had been promised, and having been given the head, left without complaint. It is possible that the king, fearful of disturbance gave a personal order that the corpse should remain where it was. It is not credible that Nicholas Carew would refuse to accede to his sister's heartbroken appeal. It seems most likely to me that Lady Ralegh did exactly as she had told her brother she would do. Quietly, under cover of darkness, the little cortège came to Beddington, where the body lies still within the Carew family vault.

There is no memorial in St. Mary's, but nor was there in St. Margaret's until 1818 when, on the strength of the one line entry in the registers, a wooden tablet was set up. The tablet, replaced by a brass in 1845 reads:

Within the Chancel of the Church was Interred
The Body of The
Great Sir Walter Raleigh, Kt.
on the Day that he was Beheaded
in Old Palace Yard Westminster.
Octr. 29th, AN. Dom. 1618
Reader—Should you reflect upon his errors
Remember his many virtues
And that he was mortal.

It was better expressed by Ralegh himself in his history of the world, the writing of which whiled away the long years of imprisonment;

> Oh eloquent, just and mighty Death! whom none could advise thou hast persuaded, what none hath dared thou has done, and whom all the world hath flattered thou only has cast out of the world and despised. Thou hast drawn together all the far-stretched greatness, all the pride, cruelty and ambition of man, and covered it all over with those two narrow words Hic jacet.

The story of Ralegh's head is even more bizarre. Bess never parted with it. Embalmed, it became, according to one account, her constant bedfellow. Unlike most Jacobean widows she never married again. Considering the intricate web of Ralegh's finances and the manner of his death, his widow seems to have been left fairly comfortably provided for. She owned, in her own name, a house in Broad Street in the City but passed much of her time in the country house of West Horsley Place in Surrey. Ralegh's principal estate had been at Sherborne, but this, Bess surrendered to the king in return for a lump sum and a pension, not always paid, of £400 per annum. One has the impression that James having pursued a personal vendetta against Ralegh was anxious to treat the family as generously as possible. A. L. Rowse has recorded some extracts of correspondence between Bess and Sir Nicholas. They are full of domestic details. Bess cannot lend her still, she has only a broken tin one but will send to London for a glass one and will do any distillation at Horsley. She will not lend him her woman to help with the preserves, he has too many green fruits. Nicholas in 1626 writes to his sister, with the calm assurance of the well-to-do, "I wonder that you will not pay the fee money at the day, which is but £20 for six months: the not paying of it will breed distrust both of yourself and of your sureties, and doth make them hasten to call in the principal". Bess may in fact have been going through some financial strain for her City house was burned down in 1623 and she had been forced to move to the parish of St. Martin in the Fields where she appears on a list with others of those refusing to pay their highway rate. Nicholas's letter comes rather ill from one who twenty years earlier had been prepared to fly the country to escape his creditors.

West Horsley Place, an imposing building of red brick, parts of which date from the time of Elizabeth I, has had a long association with the Carews. It was here that the Marquis of Exeter lived and was accused of burning that treasonable correspondence with that other Sir Nicholas in the time of Henry VIII. After their execution, the house passed to Sir Anthony Browne who succeeded Nicholas as Master of the Horse. He largely rebuilt Exeter's house. On the death of his son, in 1592, the house was purchased by Nicholas Throckmorton, Bess's brother. Sir Nicholas (Throckmorton) Carew retained ownership of the house though it was used by Bess, as we have seen, and subsequently by Carew Ralegh, her son. It perhaps explains the admonitory tone of Nicholas's letter.

Bess lived to the great age of 82, dying in 1647. It is likely that Carew Ralegh inherited the house from his uncle, along with a number of disputed legal claims dating from his father's lifetime; and from his mother the red leather bag and its grisly contents. As a family which had suffered from Stuart tyranny, Carew occupied a secure place under the Commonwealth regime. He sat as member of Parliament for Guildford and for Godalming and in 1660 was appointed Governor of Jersey. Three of his children died in the same year; they are buried in the Parish Church of West Horsley, and this perhaps induced him to sell West Horsley Place in 1665 to Sir Edward Nicholas. He died in September 1680 and was interred in the vault belonging to the Manor House where his children had been laid. Tradition, probably correct, says that the head of his father was laid in the grave with him. The relic was disturbed yet again in 1703 when a grave for the mother of William Nicholas was being dug in the same place. At last, the ghost of Sir Walter Ralegh might rest in peace, or, dare one say it, in two pieces!

CHAPTER NINE

The Civil War and After

SIR NICHOLAS THROCKMORTON CAREW, was eighty when the Civil War
began and therefore took no part in the conflict. Surrey, in any case, was closely
linked with London and saw only skirmishing between the forces of King and
Parliament. The western half of the county, under the leadership of Sir Richard Onslow,
was strongly Parliamentarian in allegiance, but there has always been a tendency for
loyalties within the county to be split between the three principal towns of Guildford,
Kingston and Croydon. Croydon landowners, perhaps because of the long association
between the town and the Archbishops of Canterbury, were Royalist to a man. The
Gardiners of Haling Manor were described by Onslow as belonging to a "dangerous
corner of malignants". It was true. Royalist Thomas Wynne of Croham Manor had his
estates sequestered by the Parliament. (This was unfortunate for Whitgift Hospital, the
owners, who had leased them to him, because the Parliamentary Commissioners ordered
that timber to the value of £200 should be felled in the park forthwith.) The Treasurer of
the Surrey Committee formed to collect funds and men to prosecute the war was Henry
Tonstall of Addiscombe Place, but he was at one time gentleman usher to Henrietta
Maria and he obviously treated his duties negligently, because in 1646 he was arrested
and ordered to account for monies with which he had been entrusted. The Lloyds and
Fromondes of West and East Cheam had even less sympathy with puritan ideals, for
they were known recusants who had long been under harassment by the pursuivants. In
1643, William Prynne, the Puritan pamphleteer, called Henry Lloyd, alias Francis
Smith, alias Francis Ryvers, alias Francis Simons, "a grand Jesuite, a great seducer and
chiefe agent in the great and damnable plot of the Gunpowder treason". A Fromonde
was for a time lay rector of Carshalton, which perhaps explains how the Vicar, William
Quelch B.D., who died in 1654 in the middle of the Cromwellian period, could boast on
his epitaph that it was his "lot through God's mercy to burn incense here about 30
years."

Wealthy merchants were finding the district a pleasanter place than "London, the
nursery of all these mischiefs". They had scant sympathy with 'King' Pym and his mobs
and still less with the "Surrey Committee for the advance of money" when it began to
assess men of property for forced loans. The eight per cent offered as interest probably
seemed a poor return for a loan whose security was "The public faith of the kingdom",
least of all in the early years when it seemed probable that the King would triumph.

For Nicholas Carew, as for many another landowner under London control, the
solution was to wait, to aid Parliament as little as possible, and to allow his sons to join
the cavalier forces. A younger son went to fight in the Second Bishops War, while his

eldest, Sir Francis, after being defeated in the election for the Borough of Blechingley in the short Parliament of 1640, continued apparently to reside at Court. This arrangement allowed the father to preserve his estates untrammelled by sequestration, while his son afforded his majesty moral and physical support at Oxford. Other Surrey landowners who followed a similar course were Sir Ambrose Browne and Sir Thomas Grymes.

So equitable an arrangement had one danger only, if the war were to be unduly prolonged, and Sir Nicholas who had for several years complained of ill health interfering with his duties as a J.P. must have been aware of it. In December 1643, he voluntarily appeared before the Committee meeting at the Greyhound, Croydon's principal inn, and added a wavering hand to an exhortation to take the National Covenant. Two months later he died. It was perhaps a last attempt to curry some favour with the Committee who might recommend the sequestration of his estates.

It is probable that Nicholas was gravely disappointed in the seven children whose kneeling figures, demure in their large ruffs, he had caused to be carved on his uncle's tomb. Mary, his youngest, and perhaps favourite, daughter, died in 1631. The Church registers call her, 'Mary, a pious daughter of Sir Nicholas Carew Knt.'. Nicholas, his second son, had set up house in his father's manor of Walton on the Hill, and it was in that parish church that his daughter, also named Mary, was christened in 1639. The registers mention that his eldest son Francis was also present, but he, himself, apparently did not attend, which is odd. The child must have died, since she received no legacy in his will, and on August 11th 1643, the father was laid to rest in Walton. The third son, George, is not heard of again after 1638 when he wrote in some excitement to say that he and the Surrey forces had joined the King in York, that the Scots had captured Newcastle, and he did not know yet how he would be used. Of Edmund, nothing is known. Then, a few weeks before the death of Nicholas came a disappointment of quite a different order to a Carew whose training led him to haggle to the last penny over any marriage portion—Oliphe, his youngest son, wrote from Cornwall to say that he had married for love!

7th July 1643

I beg you will not be displeased att mee. It is my Fortune to marry with the daughter of Sir Richard Hawkins. I confess her portion is but a hundred pounds which is more than I really deserve at her handes, but her goodness is farr beyond my deserts, but of that it doth not become me to speake. Wee do live with her ungekle Hele (?); but we must now paye him £20 per an, yet my wife hathe been alwaies with him ever since her moths death. He is aged and hath never a childe. I confess he makes very much of mee, yet it is very hard for me to pay £20 per annum out of £30. I must earnestly beg you will a little think upon mee. We were two months since in Devonshire with my brother Hawkins who is to pay my wife her portion. Hee paid me £60 and hee hath promised to pay mee the other £40 at Christmas next, as of the £60 already received I intend God willing to venture in pilchards this season either to some part of Spain or France. This at present is my prayer to Almighty God for ye safety as your healthe and once more begging forgivenesse I will ever remaine

Your obedient sonne
Oliphe Carew

It is his relations with his eldest son that are most difficult to determine. Francis had been educated at Oxford, and was married to Susan, the daughter of Sir William Romney, and is usually described as 'of Reigate' although it seems likely that he also used the Carew Manor of Ravensbury.* He was knighted some time before 1639 and seems to have been active in various parts of the county. He sat as member for

Haslemere in the Parliament of 1624, and was member for Guildford in 1627. But in 1640, when he tried for election at Blechingley, presumably as a King's supporter, he was defeated by Sir John Evelyn and Edward Bysshe, both local men. In the same year he is recorded more prosaically as defending the Carew fishing rights in the Wandle: "Sir Francis Carew twice caused Thomas Barker to be taken into custody for poaching fish between Wandsworth and Croydon". As has been said, in 1642, when the Court removed to Oxford, Sir Francis joined King Charles there, though not, it appears, to serve in the army.

This sounds like a fairly standard and useful career, yet when his father came to prepare the draft of his will he wrote: "And for that my eldest sonne Sir Francis Carew, K.B. hathe runne him selfe so farre in debte that I never could knowe nor as yet doe know the certenti of them although I have payed at several tymes farre above one thousand pounds of them . . . fearing if I should make him my executor my hole estate would be dissipated and my intent and meaning wholly frustrated for this other consideration I make and ordaine my well beloved brother in law Sir Thomas Grymes of Peckham sole executor."

One must not discount the possibility that this abuse was part of an arrangement between them, and that what he had written was for the eyes of the Surrey Committee, but it is equally possible that the tensions of war had opened a real rift between father and son. In the event the estates were left to his grandson, yet another Nicholas, who, being but nine years old, could not be blamed for taking sides with either party, although 'Sir Francys Carew (is) to have the use of them till his son is twenty-one'. None of his sons, not even the newly-wed Oliphe received a penny. Each of his servants were paid a year's wages and his granddaughters, Rebecca, Susanna, and Phyllis (Philippa?) were left £100 apiece while £3,000 was to be given to his youngest daughter Susanna as a marriage portion.

He died in February 1644 having done all that was possible to save his estates from the hands of the sequestrators. Fortunately Parliament was eager to attract back into its fold supporters of the King. A vote in April of the same year allowed confessed royalists to return to their lands, and Sir Francis Carew led many other landowners back to their estates in the Home Counties. He had attended the King as a sworn servant, but was never in the army. He had received from his father an annuity of £200, which, by reason of the great charges on his father's estate, had been unpaid during the last year. Sequestration would ruin himself, his wife, his children, and hinder his payment of his father's debts. The House of Commons Journal for 27th July 1644 notes:

> Sir Francis Carew fined £2,000, appearing to have been in service against Parliament and to have £1,000 per annum at least.

Sequestration was removed after ten days, when Sir Francis paid the first £1,000 of his fine. There was probably a real difficulty in finding the cash, for in 1645 he mortgaged his manor of Norbury to Elizabeth Castleman for £500; and two years later with the agreement of his son-in-law he mortgaged the manor of Mitcham which had previously been settled as a marriage portion on his daughter Rebecca. In 1647 his estate was re-

* This may be an error by Manning and Bray. A Francis Carew is buried in Reigate church, but he is most likely to be the son of brother Nicholas, who was baptized at Buckland. This Francis also attended Oxford University.

sequestered for non-payment of the fine. He died in 1649 with the debt still unpaid. He is buried, with three children and his sisters Mary and Elizabeth, in Reigate Parish Church.

His son, a youth of fourteen, was left in the care of Carew Ralegh. It was a good choice. The reputation of Sir Walter Ralegh soared during the Commonwealth. Not only had he been a victim of Stuart tyranny, but it was remembered also that he had served as a Member of Parliament for St. Michaels, Cornwall, and had championed the causes of his beloved west country and religious freedom (except of course for catholics). Carew Ralegh, son of the hero, was beyond criticism. He owned, in addition to West Horsley, a house in Beddington which in 1663 paid tax on eight chimneys—the biggest house in the village after Carew Manor. It may be that young Nicholas Carew and his mother occupied this during the difficult years of the Commonwealth. The strictures laid by Sir Nicholas Throckmorton Carew upon the financial capabilities of his son were doubtless fully justified; Sir Francis was not the only cavalier to ruin himself and his estate in the service of the king now executed. Moreover, each of the Carews seems to have left an accumulation of debts to be settled by his heirs; and, further, as a landowner, he was liable to meet the regular assessments that were ordered by Parliament to pay for the Civil War. The death of Sir Francis solved nothing, the estate was bankrupt, and the £1,000 had still to be paid—and by how many hundreds should it be multiplied to reach a modern equivalent? If young Nicholas was politically beyond reach, his heritage was not.

The choice was to mortgage or to lease. Lady Carew, guided no doubt by Sir Thomas Grymes, chose the latter way out and a tenant was ready to hand. On July 5th 1649 she handed over the deeds to Edward Thurland, steward of the estate of the Earl of Warwick. He endorsed them with a note that the day for the Manorial Court at Walton on the Hill was 8th August, at Wallington the 9th, and the 10th August at Norbury. Robert Rich, the second Earl of Warwick, is a likeable character. While there is no doubt of his singleminded support for the Parliamentary cause, nor of his opposition to the high-church policies of Laud, he was, exceptionally for his time, a jovial Puritan. The Earl of Clarendon refused to believe that such a man could be anything but a hypocrite, and wrote of him, "he was a man of pleasant and companionable wit and conversation, of a universal jollity, and such licence of his words that a man of less virtue could not be found out." Perhaps he acquired the freedom of speech that so offended Clarendon when as a young man he had sailed the Atlantic, being much involved with the Puritan settlements in the New World. He was for a time, President of the New England Council on which body of religious bigots he used his influence towards toleration. He thus offended both the extreme Puritans and the Court party, yet when the war came he was the obvious choice to serve Parliament as Admiral of the Fleet. In 1648, however, with the war almost over, his credit received a setback when Lord Holland, his brother, made a hare-brained attempt to rouse the men of Surrey and rescue the king from captivity. Warwick was in no way involved in the skirmishing which followed; and, when the bulk of the fleet defected to Prince Rupert, his personal popularity helped him to form another. But for all his services he could not persuade Parliament to spare his brother's life, and, in 1649, he was deprived of his office and title. He took no further part in public life and retired to the decent obscurity of Beddington, where he remained for the next four years.

The house was in a deplorable state; it had probably been little used since the death of Sir Nicholas five years earlier, and may well have been in a state of decay for years before. Cartloads of bricks, tiles, tile-pins, and nails were ordered for the running repairs necessary to keep out the weather. It is an indication of seventeenth century inflation that a carpenter now received twenty pence for each day that he worked. Particularly singled out for the work done on them were "the little house by the Mount, the Billiard house and the laundry chimney". As the warmer weather set in, it was obvious that something would have to be done to the moat if the occupants of the house were to be untroubled by their not oversensitive noses. For week after week from April to June, two, sometimes more, labourers toiled at 'lading' the moat; that is, baling it out and cleansing it of its accumulated filth; a task for which they received fifteen pence a day. As the water level fell it became obvious that the masonry facing had decayed and would need to be renewed. A 'free mason' and his assistant were procured who, with stone carted from London, and lime, sand and 'tarris'* began the repairs. Most of the labour was for cutting, squaring, and dressing the stone. While the mason was about he was set to work to make "a chimney peece in his lordshipps closeet" which had doubtless proved damp and cold during the preceding winter. Meanwhile the drawbridge was found to be unsafe and the carpenter was ordered to renew the timbers. The 'force mill', constructed by Sir Francis in the early years of the century to supply the house with water, required yet another tradesman, a mill-wright who was brought in to make necessary repairs.

The money laid out on repair work did not excuse payment of those assessments made every two or three months on the property for 'drums and colours', for the 'relief of maimed soldiers', and for the 'provision of houses of correction'–perhaps for those who had fought on the wrong side. One of the several Beddington tax collectors was Bartholomew Teg, whose family had obviously climbed higher up the social scale since his father or grandfather had been one of the labourers figuring in Thomas Mabson's accounts. The tax paid amounted to eighteen shillings and eightpence each month, a sum, again, which must be multiplied by several hundred to find an equivalent today. Against the account is written in, perhaps by the Earl himself, "besides the quartering of soldiers." It was perhaps at this point that Warwick decided to make a claim for his expenses, now totalling over £292 against the rent payable to the trustees of the young heir. The accounts were carefully written out with, for good measure, a list of other works that had been done, and "an account of moneys disburst about Beddington house for his lordshipps conveniency for which he demands nothing": these included the building of new stables, and 'the doggs kenell and yard', repairs to the Smith's forge, mending the clock and making a turret over it, putting down matting in the rooms, and making partitions with 'indores locks' and 'mending the chimneys from smoking'. The accounts were signed by Thurland and by Warwick himself. It would seem that the justice of the claim was generally recognised, although certain items, notably the chimney in the closet were marked 'un A lo' in the margin as though the trustees did not agree that this was for 'the Heires use'.

Warwick's tenancy ceased in 1653 for reasons which are not known. Before he left he had made an extension to the famous orangery providing two new iron stoves for the heating of the enlarged area, and repaired 'the fountain house'. On the whole the house was fortunate in its tenant, unlike neighbouring Croydon Palace which was sold off to Sir William Brereton, the Parliamentary general, "a notable man . . . having terrible long

---

* Tarris=tarras=trass: a volcanic earth imported to act as a cement material.

79

teeth and a prodigious stomach to turn the archbishop's chapel at Croydon into a kitchen: also to swallow up that palace and lands at a morsel". Despite his retirement, Warwick remained on friendly terms with Cromwell, whose daughter was married to Warwick's grandson. He died 19th April 1658 and was buried at Felstead in Essex. His daughter-in-law knew him better than Clarendon: she wrote, "He was one of the best-natured and cheerfullest persons I have in my time met with."

Young Nicholas Carew was 21 in 1656 but the times were probably still not propitious for moving into the mansion which seems to have been still uninhabited when John Evelyn visited in September 1658. He admired the fine old hall but spoke of 'a scambling house' and 'the first orange garden in England, being now overgrown.'

Local landowners were not the only people to suffer harassment during the Commonwealth period. The celebrated Dr. John Hacket of Cheam, whose motto "serve God and be cheerful" must have appealed to Warwick, was ordered to refrain from using the Prayer Book and was threatened by a Cromwellian soldier when he failed to do so. At Beddington the Rector, Thomas Pope, was summoned to appear before the sequestration committee. "It is ordered that Thomas Pope, Rector of Beddington and Woodmansterne in ye county of Surrey doo show cause before this Committee ... wherefore he should not be sequestered from one of ye said rectories in regard he cannot himselfe discharge ye cure of both of ye sayde Churches". The complaint was not unreasonable. He died in 1650, naming his brother, Edward Pope, Rector of Walton on the Hill, as executor. His will concludes "and withall considering these distorted times if my estate be so impaired and decayed that my said brother cannot perform this my will . . . then my will is that my wife shall be sole executrix". Pope was followed by John Cox, presumably an acceptable Puritan preacher. He died in 1669 having held his office, like the Vicar of Bray, through a series of doctrinal changes.

Throughout the Commonwealth period there was a general move to discourage celebration of the sacraments, which were thought to be Popish. Even marriages ceased to be held in church and the registers were kept only perfunctorily. In Carshalton the Rev. William Quelche felt impelled to make a general apology for the gaps that appeared in his record; but then, even before the Civil War, he had not been over punctilious. Three complete years in the marriage register read as follows:–

1640 A Londoner married Mr. Kepps sister of micham on Easter monday
1641 Mr. Meece married a couple who came from fishtead whose names he could not remember
1642 Not one marryed woe to ye vicar.

It was in 1657 that the first entry was made in the parish vestry book. The vestry was a meeting of the parishioners called by the parson, usually on Easter Monday, to elect the churchwardens for the coming year and to decide the amount of church rate to be paid. It had been meeting for perhaps two centuries, but important decisions affecting the village had up to then been taken by the Court Leet presided over by the Lord of the Manor, or his Steward. The power of manorial courts had, however, generally declined during the Tudor period and the decline was hastened by troubles of the Civil War. The vestry meeting was well equipped to take over the election of the Overseers, the levying of the poor rate and matters affecting welfare generally. Later it was able to assume control of the highways, to elect the Constable and to appoint the twin figures of village administration, the Beadle and the Parish Clerk, and so to evolve into a self-governing parish council. Other parishes found the local inn a more comfortable place in which to meet, but the Beddington vestry seems always to have met in the church.

It is characteristic that the first concern of those who made up the meeting was with their pockets. Although each parish was responsible for the care of its own poor, the good men of Beddington were determined not to be saddled with any charge from Wallington. They therefore summoned the chief ratepayers of the hamlet and required them to sign the following undertaking:—

February 12th 1657
Whereas Hugh Collett haveing fower children borne within the hamlett of Wallington, namely Jane, Mary, Leonora and Hugh, is now upon his removeall into the Towne of Beddington with his wyfe and Children. It is agreed and consented to by the inhabitants of Wallington that iff itt shall happen that the said Hugh Collett, his wyfe or any of the aforesaid children shall fall into sicknesse or poverty whereby they shall become chargeable to the towne of Beddington that the inhabitants of Wallington will indemnify the towne of Beddington from any charge that shall or may acrue to the inhabitants of Beddington on that account.

Each signed in turn, headed by John Heather, the tenant of Wallington Manor House; he was followed by Giles Hunter, William Simonds and Anthony Richardson, but the remainder were more accustomed to the spade than the pen. Nic Blarko, the overseer, made an indeterminate circle, Henry Howard and Thomas Rogger made a childish H and T as their respective marks, but Thomas Redford perhaps overcome by the occasion, dipped the quill deep into the ink, left a chain of blots across the page, dug the spluttering pen into the parchment and made a huge smudge. They need not have worried, Hugh Collett made good, and in a few years was serving as a churchwarden.

The entries were not made systematically, the rest of the page contained a list of 'Officers chosen for the year 1660'. They consist of two churchwardens, three overseers of the poor—one was Will Simonds who was at least literate, three 'Surveyours of the Highway', and Tho Pope, Constable for Wallington.

The restoration of Charles II brought a knighthood to the owner of Carew Manor, so that, once more, Beddington had a resident Sir Nicholas Carew. Although cavaliers complained about Charles's Act of Indemnity and Oblivion, saying that it meant indemnity for his enemies and oblivion for his friends, Sir Nicholas seems to have been well enough rewarded by the king, receiving a grant of Chertsey Abbey lands. John Aubrey wrote in 1673 'Of this great Abbey scarce anything remains, except the outwalls about it; out of the ruins is built a fair House which now is in the Possession of Sir Nicholas Carew, Master of Buckhounds. In front of this House are inserted two old Escocheons of Stone. Of the walls the rag-stones are a great part.' Sadly, the house has been demolished.

Carew represented Gatton in Parliament from 1661 to 1685, if it was possible to represent that Rotten Borough with its handful of voters. He also was nominated as one of the Fire Commissioners for the borough of Southwark but he does not seem to have spent much time with the court whose purpose was to hear and settle claims arising out of the town's own great fire which took place in 1676.

He married Susanna Isham, the daughter of a staunch royalist, Sir Justinian Isham, who had suffered imprisonment under Cromwell. He probably divided his time between the old-fashioned manor house at Beddington and his smart new house in Chertsey, but his name always heads the lists for the special collections that were taken regularly at the parish church and recorded in the vestry book. Collections for fires and other disasters in remote parts received very little interest; but a collection on behalf of prisoners held in

Barbary produced a very good yield, though this was exceeded by an appeal for the relief of the French Protestants in 1682. The entry for a further collection made in 1686 after the revocation of the Edict of Nantes is given in full:

Monies collected in the parish of Bedington Jan 6th 1686 toward the relief of French Protestants.

Sir Nicholas Carew	£5.	0.	0.
The Lady Carew		10.	0.
Mr. Francis Carew and Lady	£2.	8.	0.
Maddam Jane Carew		5.	0.
Maddam Phillippa Carew		5.	0.
Mr. Heather	£1.	0.	0.
Mr. John Nelme		5.	0.
Mr. Will Tomson		1.	0.
John Jones			6.
Thomas Boond			6.
Caron Here		1.	0.
Miss Barnaby		1.	0.
John Blake		1.	0.
Elizabeth Bleese			2.
Mary Polani			6.
Thomas Pope			6.
Francis Hillar		1.	0.
Widde Hillar		1.	0.
Edward Bordman			6.
Burthes Tegg			6.
Richard Herd			4.
Eliz Wood			2.
Will Wollr			6.
Thomas Fuller		1.	0.
Allin Mathow		1.	0.
Stodwan Horth			6.
Hen Gower			4.
Mris Humphries		2.	6.
Mris Dunsford		1.	0.

signed John Nelme Pastor
Charles Berriman
Churchwarden

It will be seen that Sir Nicholas had followed the now established family tradition by calling his son Francis. Sir Nicholas Carew died in 1688. Daniel Defoe includes in his *Tour through the whole island of Britain* an anecdote which is likely to refer to Francis. Having eulogised over the gardens surrounding the manor, he continues:

> I am sorry to record it to the reproach of any person now in his grave, that the ancestor of this family tho' otherwise a very honest gentleman, if fame lyes not, was so addicted to gaming and so unfortunately over-matched in his play that he lost this noble seat and parks and all the fine addenda that were then about it, at one night's play, some say at one cast of the dice, to Mr. Harvey of Coombe near Kingston; what misery had befallen the family, if the right of the winner had been prosecuted, as by what I have heard it was like to be, is hard to write; but God had

better things in store for the gentleman's posterity than he took thought for himself; and the estate being entailed upon the heir, the loser dy'd before it came into the possession of the winner and so it has been preserved and the present gentleman has not only recovered the disaster, but as above has exceedingly improved it all.

The anecdote contains all that is known of Francis Carew, who died at the early age of twenty-six and is the presumed ancestor who so nearly lost everything for his descendants.

CHAPTER TEN

An Augustan Beau

"NICHOLAS CAREW was born 1686 26th December in Covent Garden and baptized the same day". So says the entry in the registers, but it may have been entered from memory because other evidence suggests a slightly later birthday; he was probably a sickly child which explains the haste. His parents, Francis and Ann Carew, had been married for two years and had buried their first son during the previous December. Nicholas survived, and seventeen months later his sister Elizabeth was born. But, in 1689, Francis, the father, died shortly before the birth of his fourth child, who was christened Boteler, his mother's surname, and died two days later on 1st October 1689. Ann probably did not recover from the rapid succession of pregnancies; she died in 1690. It was the familiar pattern of life and death in seventeenth century London—it took four lives whilst two survived.

So Nicholas, at the age of two, became heir to the Carew estates. He and Elizabeth were brought up by their grandmother, Susanna, probably at Norbury; but their maternal grandfather, William Boteler held that he was their guardian, and claimed management of the properties. Jealousies boiled up and the two went to court, which split the lands between them and brought in a third person, Charles Bynes of Carshalton, as an official receiver. Bynes was punctilious in rendering his financial accounts but did little to maintain the properties, as John Evelyn noted in September 1700. "I went to Beddington, the ancient seat of the Carews, in my remembrance a noble old structure, capacious, and in the form of buildings in the age of Henry VIII and Queen Elizabeth; and proper to the age of English hospitality, now decaying with the house itself, heretofore adorned with ample gardens and the first orange trees that had been seen in England . . . that, standing 120 years, large and goodly trees, and laden with fruit, were now in decay, as well as the grotto fountains, cabinets, and other curiosities in the house and abroad, it being fallen to a child under age, and only kept by a servant or two from utter dilapidation. The estate and park about it is also in decay."

At the age of 18 young Nicholas purchased a small parchment-covered book with a brass clasp and wrote on the first page with many flourishes "N. Carew His book. An Dom 1705". For the next three years, between February 1705 and the 5th May 1708 he methodically entered every item of his expenditure.

When the entries begin, he is still an undergraduate at Catherine Hall, Cambridge, but his presence at that seat of learning was for social rather than educational reasons, for, on November 9th 1705, he paid his college bills and departed for London without a degree. "Expenses for leaving Cambridge Nov ye 9th 1705" he wrote and recorded a number of payments to named individuals, 11s. 6d. to his bedmaker, 5s. 0d. to 'the servants' and small sums to the cook and butler. To the college he paid a wine bill of £1 19s. 0d., a shilling for coals, and 2d. for candles. He received back from Mr. Leng, his tutor, £5 that he had deposited as "caution money" and sold his gown and surplice for £1. 10s. 0d. He had definitely finished with the academic life.

Jan ye 15 1705* I pd. to Mr Carr two and twenty pounds which I owed him for a fullbottomed wigg wch I receaved of him June ye 23 1705 and likewise a guinea for a wigg box.

The fullbottomed wig, made from real human hair, was a requirement for a gentleman; and one guesses that its acquisition marked his arrival at full independence. Twenty-two pounds was a huge sum; a working wig that he probably bought for his manservant cost far less;

My mans hat and lace	00 10 00
A wigg	01 10 00

Arriving in London he appears to have set up house for he entered:

For furniture for my house	15 00 00

Five years later he was spending much time at a house in Dover Street, and if this was where he lived in 1706 he could not have found a more fashionable quarter, for Dover Street lies between Piccadilly and Berkeley Square.
The entry is followed by:

Spent when I went for the election in Bedfordshire	20 04 6

At 19 he could hardly have stood for Parliament and one assumes that he was acting as secretary or in similar capacity for the candidate. He made occasional trips to Bedfordshire during the next three years and other places which may have been on business rather than pleasure. From the election he went to Guildford.

Spent at Guildford	01 10 00
Spent at Beddington	00 10 00
Spent at Spr Gard	00 06 06
Sp at ye christening	02 05 00
for apricocks	00 00 06

There is a pleasing random nature in the entries. If Guildford and Beddington were on business, the 6s. 6d. spent at Spring Gardens (another name for the famous Vauxhall Gardens) was strictly pleasure as was the 3s. 6d. spent at "Maribone" tea gardens and the 2s. 6d. at Mayfair. The fairly regular 6d that he spent at one or other of the coffee. houses was an obligatory item for the young man about town. Dr. Johnson wrote: "you have all manner of news there: you have a good Fire which you may sit by as long as you please: you have a dish of Coffee, you meet your friends for the Transaction of Business, and all for a penny if you don't care to spend more." Apart from the company, the attraction of the Coffee houses was the display of newspapers and journals. A Swiss traveller, de Saussure, wrote "Men will sit smoking and reading newspapers . . . talking so little you can hear a fly buzz" though he went on to say "to tell the truth [they] are not over-clean or well furnished." Nicholas used a fair cross-section of the 450 coffee houses

---

* By modern reckoning this is 1706, but England remained behind the rest of Europe until 1753 by beginning its new year on March 25th.

that flourished in town during the reign of Queen Anne. He visited Whites Chocolate House in St. James's Street, probably the most exclusive; Locks and Buttons in Covent Garden, all favourite resorts of the beaux of the day. Occasionally he went to the Grecian which was in the Strand and much used by lawyers from the Inns of Court. Here he might even have seen the great Isaac Newton who dropped in sometimes after a meeting of the Royal Society.

Like Tom Rakewell in Hogarth's Rakes Progress, he employed a French master to whom he paid £1. 13s. 6d., and a fencing master who received £10. 15. 0d. He several times paid 2s. 0d. "for finding my sword" perhaps to a 'Recovery Agency' similar to that run by Jonathan Wild who specialised in returning stolen goods to their owners, for a fee. He attended a cockpit once and spent nine shillings there; and once he lost 18s. 6d. at dice. But, with two exceptions later in his life, the amounts lost 'at play' at the dice tables rarely exceeded five shillings, and one forms an impression of a very exact young man who was sampling the fashionable pleasures rather than becoming addicted to them, and who always kept a very careful check over his expenditure.

His position obviously required that he should regularly give away small sums to charity

to a poor woman	6d.
to a letter of request	1s.
to a brief	1s.
to a fool	1s.

Nicholas clearly enjoyed music, and as a person of aristocratic rank was perhaps serenaded in various places that he visited:

Given to ye fiddlers	00 02 06
Given to ye drummers	00 02 06
Given to ye ringers	00 03 06
and Given to ye ringers at my house	01 01 06

He played on the violin, and paid 6d. for fiddle strings, and quite regularly spent 5s. 0d. at a Music Club. Yet though he went to the theatre quite often he only visited the opera once: it cost him 5s. 0d.

"September ye 25 1706" was a special day; for he wrote "I bought a pair of coach horses four years old and gave four and thirty pounds for them." Making allowances for the execrable roads, he travelled a great deal. He went to Beddington, of course; to Cambridge, to Newmarket, Hampton Court, Windsor, Richmond, Guildford and Tunbridge Wells. Perhaps for his travels, he paid £3. 9s. 6d. for a brace of pistols. Remembering what Defoe had to say about Tunbridge Wells, his expenses seem quite modest: "As for gaming, sharping, intriguing: also for fops, fools beaux, and the like, Tunbridge is as full of these, as can be desired . . . in a word, Tunbridge wants nothing that can add to the felicities of life, or that can make a man or a woman completely happy, always provided they have money: for without money a man is no-body at Tunbridge." The cost of Nicholas' trip as recorded in his little book were:

Tunbridge	
G a fool	00 01 00
Books	00 11 00
Sp taverns	00 15 00
Raffling	00 16 00

Dancing	00 01 00
Sp Oyster club	00 12 06
Lodgings	00 03 00

It is probable that up to this time he was living upon a fairly restricted allowance, but in 1707 at the age of twenty he entered into his full inheritance for he wrote:

June ye 26 1707 Left London and came to Beddington wch was ye first Day of my entrying on House Keeping an Account of my expenses from June ye 26 1707 in my House or otherwise.

The house was no doubt in a deplorable condition of neglect, and this entry is followed by a number of payments to individuals, probably servants, who were making the place ready for habitation. Then come two very large doctor's bills.

| To Dr. Radcliff | £08 12 00 |

with a later payment of £2 3s. 0d. and a further 5s. 0d. for "cupping". It sounds like a major illness, and it is in keeping with his position that he was attended by the most emminent physician of the day. One wonders whether they also talked politics:

> I sent for Radcliff: was so ill
>   That other doctors gave me over;
> He felt my pulse, prescribed his pill
>   And I was likely to recover
> But when the wit began to wheeze
>   And wine had warmed the politician,
> Cured yesterday of my disease,
>   I died last night of my physician.*

A few years later Dr. Radcliff was to retire to neighbouring Carshalton.

If the surmise that Nicholas was gravely ill during the latter part of 1707 is correct, then one can perhaps sympathise with the celebratory debauch which took place during the following February:

| Lost at play | £22 00 00 |
| Lost at play | £17 00 00 |

This is the only time that he fell victim to the fashionable vice. The next entries are purely domestic.

3 pounds of chocolet	00 12 00
a pound and half of coffee	00 13 06
3 quarters of pound of Tea	00 10 00
Blunderbuss	02 05 00

Almost the last entry in the book returned to music

| May ye 1 1708 Pd Mr Corbet for a violin | £2 10 0 |

The following year Nicholas was married to Elizabeth Hacket, the daughter of N. Hacket Esq. of South Crawley, Buckinghamshire, and he soon began to extend and modernise the mansion that had probably had its last face lift in the time of the Elizabethan Sir Francis. The voluminous Carew correspondence that was transcribed by the Rev. H. Dodd contains no reference to an architect; there is only a contract given by two village bricklayers, Henry Elkins and William Puplett, dated 1710 which refers

* Quoted by Edward Walford in Greater London

mainly to refacing the brickwork of the Great Hall, for which they were to receive £36 and two guineas in gold. It is possible that Nicholas himself designed the two deep wings that were to be added to the Elizabethan house, and that the village builders carried out the work for him. The result was sufficiently impressive to be engraved by Colen Campbell for his edition of Vitruvius Britannicus published in 1715. The house did not escape contemporary criticism, however. Daniel Defoe wrote: "It was a fine old building in Mr. Camden's time; but is now almost rebuilt from the ground by the present owner Sir Nicholas Carew who now possesses that estate . . . the house is magnificently fine; yet architects say that the two wings are too deep for the body of the house, that they should either have been wider asunder or not so long." Defoe, who wrote his account during the 1720s, goes on to say "The court before them is extremely fine and the canal in the park before the court, is so well, that nothing could be better, having a river running thro' it; the gardens are exceedingly enlarged, they take up all the flat part of the park for two or three miles; the orange trees continue, and are indeed wonderful; they are the only standard orange trees in England, and have moving houses to cover them in winter; they are loaded with fruit in the summer and the gardeners told us they have stood in the ground where they grow for above 80 years."

The critics were right. The appearance of the house was much improved by doubling the width of the wings, probably during the 1740s. The house remained in this form until the fire of 1865 which partially destroyed the south wing.

In the spring of 1710 Nicholas was sick again. His father-in-law, a prodigious correspondent, wrote in April to say how glad he was that he had "got over two troublesome distempers". The correspondence, signed "Your very affect. father" is of course one-sided. One does not know how Nicholas replied; the letters are not there. Most of them at this time are addressed to 'N. Carew Esq. In Dover Street'; perhaps because the Beddington house was in the hands of the builders. A series of letters refer to some legal business which Nicholas was being asked to conduct on behalf of friends of his father-in-law: "I will let Dymoke know and he will wait upon you the same morning in Dover Street, about nine o'clock in the forenoon, in order to go to Westminster Hall. The small pox is in many of our neighbouring towns but fewe dye." Amongst the financial and legal business an occasional personal note creeps in. In April he writes "I am grown very old for I cannot sit with less fire than at Christmas" and later he begins "Upon receipt of my Daughters letter I find ye old saying verified yt ye helping one to a servant commonly proves an unthankful office, I am sorry Tom Odell does not betake himself to his business with cheerfulness."

The young wife of Nicholas was also sick in 1710, perhaps following a miscarriage, and went to Bath to take the waters. On September 4th 1710 his sister, Elizabeth, wrote a long letter to her "deare sister Mrs. Carew at Bath", hoping that "you will finde so much benefitt that you will not resent taking the journey". Poor Elizabeth! She writes very feminine letters full of family news "My brother called here as he went by a Saturday" and laments "ye plaice does not afford so much news as ye hath . . . Aunt Carew and Mr. Hillsden diend here . . . Mr. Hackett is well he diend with us both days," and so on. The cure worked for Mrs. Carew; on 28th September, Elizabeth wrote again "I am very glad to heare ye waters agree so well with my dear sister. Dr. Colehatch is now here he tells me that same good news. I wish they may continue to do so. I find ye Dr is deeply in love with Mrs Middleton but he says the waters have not done so much good as they have done

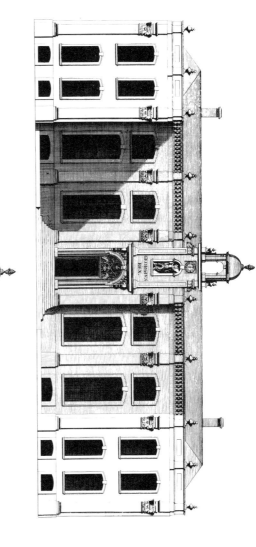
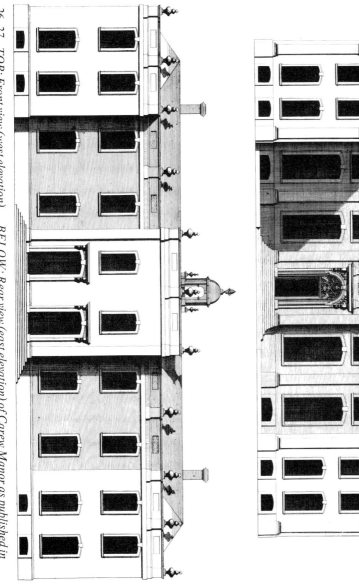

26, 27. *TOP: Front view (west elevation) BELOW: Rear view (east elevation) of Carew Manor as published in Vitruvius Britannicus by Colen Campbell c. 1715*

you, Indeed I doubt she is past cure." It could be that Bath agreed too well with her dear sister, because Elizabeth goes on "I am sorry to hear you have such bad luck at play. I have not much opportunites of trying mine as you have but in what I have it has been pretty even, except ye lottery and in that I have been very much unfortunate for all ye tickets are drawn and I have not one prize."

Nicholas was now established as one of the County gentry. In 1714 he was elected Member of Parliament for Haslemere, presumably for the Whig faction, since he was rewarded with a baronetcy on 11th August 1714 in the first honours list issued by the Hanoverian dynasty. He became Colonel of the Surrey Militia, and in 1720 was elected as a Member for Surrey. As a defender of the regime one notes that the churchwardens' accounts, May 20 1719, include a payment of 5s. 0d. "for Ringen King George birthday".

The population of Beddington was stated in 1723 to be 400, and the village, according to the curate, had no papists, nonconformist lecturers, nor meetings; although two or three families attended a Presbyterian Meeting in Croydon. The village was without a school, but two or three persons taught children to read and to sew, and poor children were sent to them and were paid for from offertory money.

The Carew correspondence has an interesting sidelight on the appointment of Rector. Ever since the Reformation the Carews, as Lords of the Manor, had been patrons of St. Mary's Church. In 1708 Nicholas had presented the living to John Leng, his tutor at Catherine Hall. The appointment suggested that he cared more for Cambridge loyalties than for the care of the souls in the parish, for Dr. Leng's other appointments included that of Chaplain to King George I, and, between 1723 and 1727, that of Bishop of Norwich, while his duties in Beddington were performed by Samuel Ley, the curate, who received probably no more than a beggarly £60 a year. In 1726 the Bishop may have considered relinquishing some of his appointments because a lady signing herself C & CC wrote to Lady Carew urging the merits of a certain Dr. Herbert, "I have an affaire of importance to press your attention. I am solicited by Lady Cartwright and Dr. Herbert to use my utmost interest to obtaining yr Ladyships approbation and consent for Dr. Herbert's being at Beddington. She assures me he is a perfectly good sort of man. I am sure he is a pretty one, has charming teeth when he speaks and a sweet voice and he protests was he to come to the living without the approbation of his patron and family he should be the most anxious creature upon earth, but on the contrary could he be so happy as to obtain yr favour in the case, it shall be his endeavour to do your ladyship whatever service lies in his power." It appears that the Lord Chancellor is also urging his suit, but that so far Nicholas had refused to consider him. She assures her reader that the only interest he has out of two other posts is that Beddington is nearer to town, "which he desires".

In 1727 the Bishop caught smallpox while attending the coronation of George II, and expired. Dr. John Herbert became Rector of Beddington, but the patron from whose hands he received the living was not Nicholas but the new King. Nicholas must have died very suddenly, because there is no other way that a man so careful over his finances could die without making a will. The result for Beddington was no doubt tragic; the heir to the estates was once more a child of seven.

In 1770 Beddington was visited by that inveterate gossip Horace Walpole who could himself trace a descent from "Sir Nicholas Carew whose head, as he was Master of the Horse and knight of the Garter flew off (A.D. 1539) in one of the moods of Henry VIII." He says also that he saw there "a mezzotint of Sir Nicholas Carew, who lived temp. George I and who never did anything but sit for that print." Not for the first nor the last time was "Horry" very wrong!

28. *Sir Nicholas Carew 1687-1727, 1st Baronet*

29. *Facsimile 18th century wrought-iron screen in front of Carew Manor, surmounted by the arms of Sir Nicholas Carew, 1st Baronet (see also page 116)*

CHAPTER ELEVEN

Decline. Sir Nicholas Hacket Carew

S OME OF the virility had gone out of the Carew stock. They no longer produced the large families of earlier times and the terrible toll of infant mortality was only a little improved; of the male heirs since Sir Nicholas Throckmorton Carew, three died in their forties, one at fifty-three, and one at twenty-six. Of the four children born to Nicholas and Elizabeth, two survived them; a son, christened Nicholas Hacket, and a daughter, Ann, who married her cousin Thomas Fountain, but died childless. The new heir had only daughters; Elizabeth who died in childhood, and Catherine, who outlived her father by seven years, dying unmarried in 1769. She was the last of the direct line. The blighting of the famous orange trees in 1739 was a paradigm of the extinction of this once so fruitful family.

The sudden death of Nicholas in 1727 left problems for his wife. The diversification of Carew interests, though shrunken since Tudor times were such that a cool business head was needed to control them. Lady Elizabeth re-married to William Chetwynd (who seems to have been her steward) and they jointly managed the estates on behalf of her son. In lands, Beddington, and Bandon (still listed separately)with Norbury and Walton on the Hill formed the principal block of territory, while Elizabeth held Banstead and the wealden manors of Horne and Burstow for life, probably as part of her marriage settlement. Then, in further augmentation of their income, the family owned farms and houses in Croydon, Mitcham, Streatham, Carshalton, Morden and Merton; while, as part of the expanding commerce of the early eighteenth century, Nicholas had purchased slave-worked plantations and iron works in the New World.*

Nothing of special interest has come to light concering the minority of Sir Nicholas Hacket Carew, Baronet. Lady Elizabeth did not long enjoy the beautiful teeth of Dr. Herbert who died within three years of coming to Beddington. She died in 1740, a year before her son came of age. One guesses that as a young man of fortune he dipped into the fashionable dissipations of the age far more freely than his father had ever done but at the age of twenty-one he married Katherine Martin of Overbury in Worcestershire, her family wisely insisting that as part of the marriage arrangements he should settle the sum of ten thousand pounds upon her; or, if she should die, upon her daughter. Her first

---

* The American property is first mentioned in the will of Sir Nicholas Hacket Carew, but he was a spender, not an investor and I assume therefore that his father was the purchaser.

daughter was christened Catherine on 20th May 1742, and, three years later, a second daughter, Elizabeth, followed; but no more children were born to the young couple.

Sir Nicholas Hacket Carew was responsible for some rebuilding of the ancestral home. It was probably he who doubled the width of the wings, though the north wing was almost at once devastated by fire, and left unfurnished and unrepaired. In this state it was seen by the lord of Strawberry Hill. "It is an ugly place with no prospect, a large very bad house, but it was burnt, wretchedly rebuilt after the Restoration and never finished. Nothing remains of the ancient fabric but a brave old hall with pendant roof copied by Wolsey at Hampton Court, a vast shield of arms and quarterings over the chimney, and two clumsy brazen and irons which they told us had served Queen Elizabeth in the Tower, but looked more as if they had served her as cannon to defend it." Other visitors were less scathing, "As we look at the noble facade of the old mansion, our gaze wanders to the northern wing, and we recall the story once current that this portion of the hall was haunted by beings who were not of this world. It used to be said that the north wing had never been completed, owing to the pranks of some mischievous spirits or goblins, who pulled up the boards of the floor as often as they were nailed down. Often in the long bygone time, have I, when crossing the park, turned my eyes with a curious interest towards the farther wing of the hall, where darkness and desolation seemed to confirm the ghostly tradition. The windows were bare of curtain and blind; no human being was ever seen at them; no light ever gleamed from them during the hours of darkness." The Rev. Daniel Lysons has also left a more prosaic description that is less impregnated with gothic gloom. "In this hall," he writes, "is a portrait of a lady mistakenly shown as Queen Elizabeth . . . A small room adjoining the hall retains the ancient panels with mantled carving; over the chimney is a small portrait of one of the Carews, surrounded by a pedigree. Another room has several portraits of the Hacket family; among these is a good portrait of Bishop Hacket, said to be by Sir Peter Lely. In a parlour at the north end of the hall are some other family portraits, the most remarkable of which is that of Sir Nicholas Carew who was beheaded in the time of Henry VIII, painted on a board." The south wing contained the dining and drawing rooms, and other large apartments, together with a long gallery that extended through its entire length.

Like his father, Sir Nicholas Hacket Carew was colonel of the Surrey Militia, but he found it less of an empty honour than it had been in the earlier, more peaceful epoch. Englishmen prided themselves on being an unmilitary nation, they had a deep suspicion of armies and a poor opinion of soldiers. There was only one reason why a man should become a soldier, and that was abject poverty. Even during a national emergency like Bonny Prince Charlie's invasion, Lord Onslow's attempts to raise a Surrey regiment had proved so unpopular that the force was woefully under strength and never saw active service.

In 1757 the country was once more embroiled in a war that was being fought in India and Canada as well as on the continent of Europe, and there was a real fear that while our regular forces were abroad the French might try to invade Britain. William Pitt the Elder rushed through Parliament a bill that would call the county militia into being for home defence. Lord Onslow, as Lord Lieutenant of the county and Carew, his deputy, had the responsibility for mustering the militia in their respective areas, by calling for volunteers, if possible, but otherwise by a ballot of all males between the ages of 18 and 50. It was the intention of the bill that those called should be free to carry on with their normal work, and spend only a few days each summer at drill. A proposal that they should drill on Sundays was rejected as irreligious.

The raising of a county regiment proved just as unpopular as during the '45 emergency, despite the many classes who were able to claim exemption from the ballot. Peers and parsons, soldiers and schoolmasters, seafaring men and Crown employees, poor men with more than one legitimate child, serving members of the universities, and Thames watermen could all claim to be exempt under the act, and that their names should not go into the ballot. The Guildford mob, says Walpole, chased 'Speaker' Onslow in his coach for fifteen miles until he promised to take no further steps till the next Parliament. The eastern half of the county showed an equal antipathy to military service, as Carew and his fellow justices discovered when they arrived at the Greyhound in Croydon to carry out the ballot. The following excerpts are from a letter which he wrote to Lord Barrington, the Secretary at War:

"We . . . being met at Croydon . . . for hearing the appeals of all Persons Aggrieved by being inserted in the List of Persons proper to serve—Persons to the number of between five and six Hundred in a Riotous manner armed with long staves, Bludgeons and other Offensive Weapons met and insisted on entring the Room where we were so Assembled and that we should not proceed with the Ballot that day, upon which we desisted and were obliged to postpone the Ballot until the next Day." Having drawn the names and handed the lists to the Constables to bring in the men for swearing, they heard that an even bigger mob, including men from neighbouring Kent, were threatening the peace on the day appointed and had "prepared themselves in a most hostile manner". They asked that Lord Barrington despatch a company of foot soldiers to join the troops of dragoons already in the town "to protect Us from all Insults from the Populace . . . and prevent an infinite Deal of Mischief to the Persons and Properties of

His Majesty's most faithfull subjects
Nicholas Carew
Saml Atkinson
John Heathfield

Oct 5th 1757"

Holding the ballot was only the start of Carew's troubles; in towns like Croydon and Southwark there were many bolt-holes and alleys into which the Constables did not care to penetrate, and even when they brought in the men selected for service, recruits were excused if they were able to find a substitute, or if they paid a £20 exemption fine, of which £10 went to the military and £10 to their parishes. Keeping the men together was a further problem; even regular soldiers did not live in barracks, but were quartered upon innkeepers and local householders according to registers of accommodation kept by the justices. The innkeepers were particularly vocal about their rowdy unwished-for guests, who with their horses, filled up their available space. Nor could they resist charging at the very highest rate for food and provender consumed. Companies based on Croydon were spread in inns over the whole area from Cheam to Mitcham and Coulsdon and the men had to march many miles for parades and for training. The officers, chosen from men of property within the county, were equally lacking in military experience while the diffusion of their men made discipline almost impossible. In the towns the men absconded almost as fast as they could be enrolled and paid.

Then the Commanding Officer had to deal with quarrels amongst his officers, drunken rowdyism from his men and fights and complaints from innkeepers and tradesmen. A Richmond shoemaker who had supplied new shoes to an officer of the 54th Foot wrote "he told me he would come on the Morrow & Pay me for the Shoes & return my Buckles which the amount of both is Eight Shillings to much for me to lose as I have a Large Family & no Income but my own Labour to Support them & as he hath left the town above this Fortnight past and I can get no intelligence of him . . . I hope you will not let me remain with the Loss". This letter has been preserved only because the shoemaker wrote to the Secretary at War; how many similar complaints went to the Commanding Officer and the Justices we can never know. The Justices themselves were often only half-hearted, "A quibbling Justice of the Peace" refused to honour a billeting order because "of the S being wanted in the word Tooting". He claimed that as there was an Upper and a Lower Tooting, the order should "be Granted in one of the Tootings".

There were other worries for Carew apart from his military difficulties. The day of the old-fashioned squire was drawing to its close. The acres of deer park, the far flung commons and perhaps even the demesne farm, brought very little return in the way of hard cash. The additions he had made to the mansion were expensive and unlike more progressive landlords there is no evidence that he took any interest in land and stock improvement. The management of his estates he left entirely to his steward, who was, it seems, as unbusinesslike as his master. Then, at the peak of his concerns with the regiment, Catherine, his only surviving daughter, fell sick. The malady is given no name, but the condition was declared to be incurable, and the desperate parents tried the only palliative known to the eighteenth century, the waters of an inland spa, not fashionable Bath but quieter Malvern. "I have heard that the waters here sometimes perform wonderful cures" as Lady Carew wrote to her friend Lady Isham. "I pray that I shall not have the loss of an only child to add to the afflictions I find myself ill able to struggle with . . . Sir Nicholas left us on Monday . . . I am grieved to say his affairs are sadly perplexed and he involved in great difficulties and I know not what hands he may fall into, indeed my heart bleeds for him, I well know he can ill support a change of fortune, seeing him so distressed."

The Malvern waters performed a minor miracle for Catherine; she did not die, and by June 1759 Carew was able to report that his regiment was ready for action. It was truly his now as Onslow had handed over the management of his unwilling troops and Sir Nicholas was sole colonel of the Surrey Militia. The men, at least on parade, looked like soldiers in their red coats, breeches, and white gaiters, with their powdered hair tied neatly back into a regulation 'queue' beneath their tricorne hats. The sergeants were resplendent in their sashes, and the twenty-five officers, mounted and equipped at their own expense, included most of the younger county gentry. Apart from a stack of unpaid bills the regiment was complete. They were embodied into the regular army and were ordered to take up stations in the Thames estuary; the move would at least take them away from the vexations of their creditors.

Carew's pride as he rode at the head of his troops was not unmixed with anxiety, lest discipline should break down on the line of march. He had impressed upon his officers

30. Opposite: The Hall about 1740. This is an imaginative reconstruction drawn nearly a century later by Joseph Nash

that they were to pass through a number of 'nice towns' and expressed a hope that they would accompany the men. There is no reason to suppose that the good men of Dartford, Gravesend and Rochester were any more eager to be defended by the Surrey regiment than were the innkeepers of Croydon, Beddington, and Carshalton, and it was certain that the problems of a regiment spread across the countryside would be repeated in the new billets. Moreover a painful swelling in his ankle made his temper even more unpredictable than usual.

In the event it proved hopeless to control the men, and Carew received permission to split the unit into two battalions, with George Onslow, young nephew of Lord Onslow, in charge of the companies at Gravesend and Dartford. Then, whatever pride of command he may have felt was shattered when the pain spread from the ankle to the whole foot and proved to be that arch enemy of eighteenth century bon viveurs–the gout!

Colonel Carew had perforce to make an agonising return to Beddington in a jolting coach. There, Nicholas Dunbar, his second in command, wrote to him in a mood of pleasant banter which turns to serious complaint:

1760

Dear Sir Nicholas

The Notion I form to myself of yr appearance at this time is that of an Eastern Prince placed under a Canopy of State ready to receive Sovereign ambassadors and the addresses of some of his inferior neighbours. I think I see you placed with your gouty leg in an Elbow or Easy chair wrapt up in flannel as big as my body with my Lady, Miss Carew and Mrs. Robinson all about you sitting as grand as an Emperor and as peevish as an old woman, they afraid to move and to speak and you repenting your too liberal and high living in the days of your youth; O Claret! says Sir Nicholas, O Gravy Sauces! High seasoned Victuals! But above all O the pleasures of 12 oclock at Night to two or three in the morning. Must I give you all up or be tormented in this manner? I told you when you were bandaging your ankle at Rochester that it was all useless. I knew it was the prelude to what you now have.

I hope in a little time to have the honour of bowing to yr Honour under your Canopy and wishing you much joy of this new acquired sign of long health and long life. Thus far I write to you as Sir Nicholas Carew a good honest County Gentleman, laid up with gout, what follows is as a military man at the head of a Regiment.

I gave you Sir, about five weeks ago, the Bill for shoes, the bill for breeches Etc. due to Mr. Lewis, & a bill of £15 or so of a poor man, who furnished stockings of that value to your Regiment, when I gave you these Bills in my room here, you would not be at the trouble to sign them tho you had nothing to do but to put your name to them. You took them with you & said you would return them signed to me in a day or two. Yet I have never seen them, nor heard anything about them.

That poor fellow to whom the £15 is due, to my certain knowledge has borrowed the sum two or three times over and now swears he will arrest me because it was I that bespoke them.

Pray Sir Nicholas have you no compassion to the wants & necessities of others? Consider this poor man's credit depends upon the money & if he arrest me I cannot be surprised at it.

Another arrest I am threatened with for the Sergeant's sashes £21. 0. 0. I bespoke them by your order. I know no fund to pay them. I am sure Smithe wont pay them out of the Clothes money, and as Matters are managed by you and Glover. I am afraid this is not the only sum that at the last will fall heavy upon the Colonel & must be paid out of the rents of Beddington & out of his own private finances all these articles you must charge to the Honour of being Colonel of the Militia.

Nicholas Dunbar

The financial crises continued. Amongst the Carew correspondence is a note, unsigned and undated, but addressed to Sir Nicholas Carew. It is even less delicate than Dunbar's epistle.

I now give you up. I knew what your Dilatoriness in Business would bring you to, you and your steward neither of you will ever touch one sixpence of that money. The Clerk looked over the returns and hugged himself with the large savings that would be. They are fine pickings when they have to deal with Fools and Children.

On March 18th 1762 Catherine, Lady Carew, died; she was forty-one. The loss of his wife; the exigence of his affairs; worries over his regiment, soon to be disbanded, caused Carew's fortitude, never overstrong, to give way. On 8th August, having completed his will, he was laid beside her in the Carew vault.

The long and complicated will shows the range of his interests and the disarray into which they had fallen. The Manor of Banstead, with his properties in Horne and Burstow, had, for the last ten years, been mortgaged to his wife's uncle from whom he had additionally borrowed very heavily. He had borrowed further large sums from his brother-in-law, and the interest on these loans had never been paid. He had begun negotiations for the sale of Banstead, together with a house in Wallington called Old Manor, to Roland Frye, a retired West Indian planter. Frye probably needed the Wallington residence because the manor house at Banstead, which had once housed Edward I, had crumbled into dust during the two centuries that the Carews owned it. By the long-standing agreement with his Martin in-laws, he was required to settle £10,000 upon his daughter Catherine, (it was probably the sum that his wife had brought as a marriage settlement) and she was to be allowed to occupy, but not to inherit, the Beddington mansion house. He directed that his many debts should be paid off by the sale of his outlying English and American properties, and hoped that by so doing the historic holding, including the family mansion house with its furniture, plate and pictures, could be maintained in good repair. On Catherine's death the estate was entailed upon the eldest son of his cousin the Rev. Dr. Fountain, Dean of York; or, if he had no living male issue (as proved to be the case) to the eldest son of Richard Gee of Orpington, who was to assume the name and arms of Carew.

Then follows a curious passage:

Whereas my daughter through the visitation of God is become very infirm in Body and if she should marry it will bring dishonour to her family Now for the prevention of which I do hereby direct that in any case she ... shall marry ... in such case she shall ... immediately loose the said annuity and benefits given to her ... and be as if she was naturally dead.

What was the malady whose secret must never be known? The disability had shown itself when Catherine was fifteen and Lady Carew had made her trip to Malvern. It is possible that the females of the family were consumptive, but this romantic condition was no bar, in eighteenth century terms, to marriage. Was there some irregularity of sexual functioning, accompanied perhaps by mental instability? Was this the thing that was too shameful ever to be known?

Catherine survived her father by seven years and carried the secret of her dishonour to the grave. She died, unmarried, in 1769. According to the will of her father, Beddington was to pass to the eldest son of his cousin Rev. Dr. John Fountain, the Dean of York, but not until he was 25. The heir died in 1780 without reaching the age of inheritance. During all this time, and while the necessary Acts of Parliament were passed to unscramble the estates, William Pellatt remained in control.

31. The Rev. Bromfield Ferrers, Rector 1783-1841

With the eclipse of the Carews, the incoming rector dared to raise that longstanding bone of contention between the parson and his patron, the Beddington Portion. Ever since the Reformation the tithes on two hundred acres of land north of the river had been payable not to the rector, as was his due, but to the Lord of the Manor. The Rev. John Bromfield Ferrers, who came to the parish in 1783, found that he was expected to pay rent of £2. 3s. 4d. and "to deliver yearly at the barn door in the yard of the Mansion House at Beddington all the tythe straw of wheat and rye arising in the parish, 7 quarters of wheat, 4 of rye and 30 of barley, and the rector granted the patron all the tythe of oats growing in the parish except on the glebe lands."

Earlier rectors had disputed the payment, notably in 1703 during the minority of Sir Nicholas (d. 1729) and again in 1752 and a compromise situation had been arrived at. Now Ferrers flatly refused to pay up, and the ensuing case of Pellatt v. Ferrers proved to be a field day for the lawyers and incidentally for the local historian. It was discovered that the matter had been fully investigated in the year 1473, when the Rector and the Portionier were at loggerheads over tithes from these same lands, then known as 'Huscarle's Fewd'. At the Bishop of Winchester's command, the ecclesiastical lawyers not only took statements from the oldest inhabitants of the time, but had found amongst their parchment rolls records of a still earlier enquiry that had been heard before the Archdeacon of Surrey in 1309. This time it was the Abbott of Bermondsey who was in dispute with the Portionist. The court of 1789 having heard the evidence decided that as the earlier enquiries had only established that the institution of Portionist was an ancient one without finding evidence of its foundation, that judgement should be given in favour of the Rector.

Any jubilation felt by Ferrers was dispelled in 1801, however, when a counter petition on behalf of the Carews was heard. It concerned the ancient house just south of the church, with its gardens and orchard which he believed to be his own rectory, but which it now appeared had been the subject of various exchanges with Sir Richard Carew, and was beyond doubt the one-time dwelling of the Beddington Portionist. Further, it had been granted by Elizabeth I to Sir Francis Carew.

The Rev. Bromfield Ferrers removed his personal belongings into lodgings in Wallington perhaps wondering why he had ever begun the dispute.

CHAPTER TWELVE

Winds of Change

THE REVOLT of the Rector was symptomatic of the changes that were taking place in the structure of village society so close to the metropolis during the latter half of the eighteenth century. The forelock-pulling peasantry were being edged out by a new gentry whose acreage may have been smaller than that held by the traditional Lords of the Manor, but whose wealth in real terms was far greater. As the population of London reached its first half million (about 1750) the merchant classes followed the aristocracy in moving out of the smoke, noise, congestion, and stench of the city into the villages round about. Epsom, Ewell, and Carshalton still have many fine residences, both large and small, built during this period by the bankers, lawyers, and merchants who were escaping from "the serpentine narrow streets, close dismal long lanes, stinking alleys, dark gloomy courts, and suffocating yards" to breathe the pure air that blew from Banstead Downs and to drink the unpolluted water flowing from the springs of Wandle. Often the country house was only a place of relaxation from the suffocating town office.

> So merchant has his house in town
> And country seat near Banstead Down
> From one he dates his foreign letters,
> Sends out his goods and duns his debtors;
> In t'other in his hours of leisure,
> He smokes his pipe and takes his pleasure.
>
> Prior

The limit on development was the state of the roads leading back to Town. The Act for Amending Roads on the south side of the Metropolis was passed in 1718 and had made turnpikes to Epsom, Croydon and Sutton; and if the development of Beddington lagged behind these places it was not only because the Carews held most of the land, but because of the appalling state of Beddington and Croydon Lanes through which one had to pass to reach the turnpike.

Not all the mansions, however, were inhabited by Londoners; many belonged to manufacturers whose factories lined the banks of the River Wandle. In 1610 this fast-flowing little river had turned the wheels of no fewer than 25 corn mills along its nine miles of length. By 1750 the industries had proliferated to include calico printing, leather mills, copper working, paper manufacturing, and snuff grinding, as well as the traditional corn mills. The bleaching of calico was well established at Wallington and Carshalton and was soon to take over the palace of the archbishops in Croydon. By 1800, forty industries were established in the Wandle valley, making it the busiest river for its size

32. *The final appearance of the baroque manor house from a lithograph by Joseph Nash c. 1830*

33. The manor house as seen from the garden, from a lithograph by Joseph Nash c.1830

in the kingdom. As England groped towards the modern age, the aristocratic landlords with their deer parks and vast land-holdings were, at least in this corner of Surrey, becoming an anachronism. By the late 1700s, the empty Carew manor house had as rival at least six mansions in Beddington, and four in Wallington, while Carshalton was, as Defoe says, "one of the most beautiful spots south of London . . . [with] many handsome houses; some built with such grandeur and expense that they might be rather taken for the seats of nobility than the country houses of citizens and merchants".

The favourite promendade of this new society was Ladye Walk. In this grove, hallowed by memories of Queen Elizabeth, the ladies and gentlemen took the air after their early dinner hour. The Rev. John Williams paints a pleasing picture of the ladies in their crinolines, and gentlemen in plum-coloured coats, pink satin waistcoats, and breeches and white stockings leading their lap dogs along the gravelled path. Between the trees lining the high ridge the evening sun glowed upon the cultivated fields worked in the immemorial pattern of their Saxon ancestors. They watched the peasants in round straw hats and smocks returning wearily from their labours, bound for home or the Plough Inn. Their poise, the elegance of the furnishings in their comfortable homes, and the peace of the rural life far removed from the London mobs chanting for "Wilkes and Liberty", made their world safe and secure; the age of reason could last for ever.

The village was soon to have a new squire, for there were still living descendants of the Carew stock. The Sir Nicholas who died in 1688, had, in addition to the short-lived Francis, a daughter named Philippa who was probably the 'Aunt Carew' with whom Elizabeth had 'diend'. She was married to Richard Gee, a gentleman of Orpington, and in 1780, her grandson, another Richard, received the estates with royal licence to take upon himself the name and arms of the proud family.

Richard Gee Carew has received a bad press. He was of miserly habits; the old coat which he habitually wore was found on his death to be lined with banknotes; he was, according to Bentham, Miser Farebrother, the villain of a story by Farjeon in the Illustrated London News, and he had a habit, very exciting for his successors, of hiding sums of money about the house. He was a bachelor, possibly lonely, and probably made to feel an outsider by Beddington society. He also had an interest in history, and published a selection of his family correspondence in *Archaeologia*.

The new occupant of Carew Manor, with his shapeless jacket, was not the only shock for the satin-clad beaux with their powdered hair. Revolution was in the air, and the rise of Napoleon brought menace even to rural Surrey. The militia was again embodied as a full-time regiment, while the Surrey Yeomanry brought a dash of scarlet and light blue to enliven the disputes over billeting. For the adventurous there were the Croydon Cavalry or Wimbledon Light Horse, volunteer soldiers whose military effectiveness was far exceeded by the splendour of their uniforms. In July 1799 the king held a massed review on Wimbledon Common of 676 cavalry and 1,958 infantry that the county had raised for defence of the realm.

More useful was the world's first public railway, proposed in 1801, and opened in 1803, between Wandsworth and Croydon. The route followed the Wandle valley, and had short spurs connecting it to the many mills, including those at Beddington Corner and Hackbridge. The railway was, of course, horse drawn and was open for use by anyone who paid the tolls and whose cartwheels fitted the gauge of the plateway. Two years later a southward extension was opened that continued the line as far Merstham, along the south eastern border of the parish in Smitham Bottom. Nelson's victory at Trafalgar rendered the planned continuation to Portsmouth unnecessary, and the southern line never paid its way. At the time it was regarded as a scientific wonder, and sporting gentlemen laid wagers on the total weight that could be hauled by a single horse.

One summer Sunday morning, worshippers found a poster attached to the church door. It gave notice that the bill for the enclosure of **Beddington** had received the royal assent on 22nd July 1812, and gave the names of the three commissioners who had been appointed to carry out the tasks involved. They were Joseph Rennington of Godstone, George Smallpeice of Stoke next Guildford, both landowners, and a lawyer, Thomas Bainbridge, from Middlesex. The system of strip farming was wasteful of labour, uneconomic, and did not lend itself to the improved farming techniques that had been developed, mainly during the preceding century. To group them into working farms made good economic sense. There was also a great deal of rough uncultivated ground, both on the agriculturally inferior sandy soils that occurred in patches on the south of the village, as well as lands in the north on the old Beddington Marsh. To enclose them and convert them into viable units was the chief aim of the bill.

The actual landholders in the parish were few; many had already made sensible exchanges of their strips to consolidate them into more compact blocks that obviated the time wasted in passing from strip to strip scattered across the open fields. Providing they could meet the cost of enclosing their holdings they would lose nothing. The only sufferers by enclosure would be the poor. The commons and wastes, by custom, provided even those who had no stake in the soil with brushwood for fuel, bracken for bedding, reeds for thatch, rabbits and birds for the pot, and wild berries for pies. On them their chickens might scratch, geese and goats find provender. Helped out by the produce of their cottage gardens, families might live on the shilling and sixpence a day that was the going rate for a day labourer, especially if his wife could obtain a few days weeding at tenpence a day, and his children earn two shillings a week scaring the birds from other men's crops. Enclose the commons, substitute a rent on the five acres that the commissioners allocated 'for the poor' to be spent on 'seconds bread' for free distribution to those in need and one can see how it was that while the farmers and plum-coated gentry groaned about the amounts they were compelled to disgorge as poor rate, the real quality of life for the labouring masses became increasingly impoverished. Beddington was not unique. Cheam and Sutton lost their commons at about the same time, and Croydon some twenty years earlier. Between 1796 and 1815, more than eighteen hundred Enclosure Acts were passed by Parliament, to the great improvement of agriculture, and the increasing pauperisation of those who worked at it.

When the commissioners came to define the northern boundary of the manor they met with unexpected objections from the commoners of Mitcham who claimed that 200 acres of their land was being absorbed into the Beddington enclosure. The boundary had probably been a matter of dispute for years; it is recorded that Agnes Huscarle in 1239 carried on a series of lawsuits with the Prior of Merton over common pastures. To village rivalries belongs the jingle:

> Sutton for Mutton
> Carshalton for Beef,
> Croydon for a pretty girl
> And Mitcham for a thief.

106

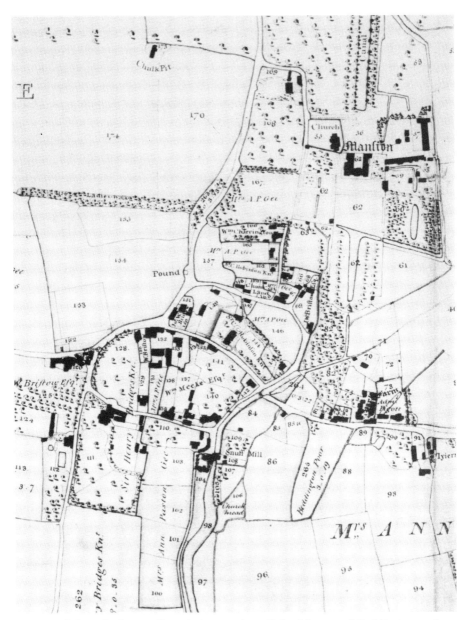

34. Detail from Inclosure Commissioners plan of the Manors of Beddington and Bandon

During the seven years of legal argument, won eventually by the men of Mitcham, the miser of Beddington died, bequeathing his lands to the widow of his brother William, Mrs. Anne Paston Gee. So, when the final allocation was made, it was Mrs. Gee who received 676 acres or about four-fifths of the total. Of the remaining fifth, 81 acres was allocated to J. Bristow of a family of lawyers; seven to Sir Henry Bridges, a gunpowder manufacturer of Ewell; and 34 acres went as glebe to the Rector. Sir Christopher Robinson, an Admiralty lawyer; Admiral Piggott; and W. Meek owned houses and gardens in the centre of the village. It left very little for the other nine holders to share. There was still less for the other one thousand one hundred and forty who made up the population of the parish.

The bequest to Mrs. Anne Paston Gee disappointed the hopes of a certain Mr. Pritchard, an illegitimate son of William Gee, who attended Cambridge and took holy orders, and had reason to expect a substantial legacy, and who now found himself disowned. He published his complaint in a pamphlet entitled *The adopted son; or, 20 years at Beddington.*

The Rev. T. Bentham, writing in 1923, was able to recall conversations with people who had known Mrs. Gee. "Old Mr. Lambert . . . who died some years ago at the age of 82 was then a small child. His father was tenant of the snuff-mill, and also churchwarden to Mr. Ferrers. He told me that as a boy he was taken down to the house at Christmas and was given a sovereign by Mrs. Gee, next year he received two sovereigns, the third year three sovereigns and so on. He used to hope that Mrs. Gee would live for ever, but alas, his golden visions were blotted out by her death a year or two afterwards in 1828. There was no more sincere mourner for Mrs. Gee than Mr. Lambert. He describes her as a little dark woman with ruddy cheeks and a pleasant expression. She used to be carried to church on Sundays in a Sedan chair by four of her labourers in clean white smocks." Her steward was John Ashby, who lived in a house near the fords and had shooting rights over the whole estate almost to himself, and fishing in what was still one of the best trout streams in England. "Every year it was the custom to clean out the mud from end to end. Every year too, the lake in front of the house was netted and the trout carried to restock other parts of the river."

While Richard Gee Carew was creeping around his lonely mansion, a much more colourful figure was making a name for himself on the high seas. Sir Benjamin Hallowell was born in Canada in 1760. He entered the navy at the age of twenty-one and served chiefly in the Mediterranean. He commanded a ship, the *Swiftsure,* at the battles of St. Vincent and Aboukir Bay, and it was he whose ship attacked and captured the French flagship *L'Orient.* He had the curious conceit of ordering a coffin to be made from the mainmast of the prize which he presented to his admiral, Lord Nelson, as a reminder, surely unnecessary, of the mortality of man, and with the hope that though he might not need it for many years, he could now rest within one of his own trophies. The gift was accepted without rancour and the hero kept it, even going to look at it once more on the day that he sailed away on the Victory to his death.

Sir Benjamin was a man of huge stature, able to quell a mutiny with his bare fists. He was promoted to Rear-admiral in 1811, and in 1815 was created Knight Commander of the Bath. The latter years of his service were spent with the home fleet from which he retired as Admiral in 1830. In 1828 his cousin Mrs. Gee died, and he received the Carew estates, bringing more distinction to the manor than was apparent in some of the more

35. Sir Benjamin Hallowell Carew. Inherited Beddington 1828 died 1834

recent holders. "Half as much twenty years ago had indeed been a blessing" he growled, "but now I am old and crank."

With the estates he adopted the name of Carew, but lived only six years to enjoy them. He was succeeded by his eldest son Charles Hallowell Carew. It would seem that the holders inherited some of the ill luck that killed off the original family, for Captain Charles Hallowell Carew died in 1849 at the age of forty-seven, leaving an heir, Charles Hallowell Hallowell Carew aged only eighteen. It may have been that "Charlie" Carew, (Buster to his racing associates) did not inherit an estate in full running order. As Lady Bracknell said "Land gives one position and prevents one from keeping it up." The grove of beeches that had shaded Queen Elizabeth was felled in 1835; an act of vandalism that provoked Miss Charlotte Cookson to eighty-six lines of anguished iambic pentameters

> The Village pleads in vain; the Doom is past
> And thou, sweet Grove art sacrificed at last;
> Thy graceful line of variegated shade,
> That crowned the summit of the far-spread glade,
> O'er which the sun of centuries has been shed,
> And countless moons their silvery lustre spread,
> O'er which the storms of Ages rushed in vain,
> Destroying Man has levelled with the plain.

The deer from the home park were sold off in 1852. "Charles Carew", says Bentham charitably, "had in his youth fallen into the hands of moneylenders and was never able to disentangle himself from their clutches." Later writers have been more direct, the 'moneylenders' were in fact bookmakers, and "Charlie" found himself faced with debts that amounted to £350,000. He had an idea, which has occurred to others since, that if he placed all his available cash upon a horse to win, it would solve his financial problems. The horse lost, and bankruptcy proceedings were instituted in 1857. Even this procedure was not a simple one; it required an Act of Parliament to execute the disentailing of the estate and its mortgages, and to settle a legal wrangle.

The manors of Beddington and Norbury were sold by auction in 1859. The lands at Norbury were purchased by William Goldsmith, who was the then tenant of the property. The northern portion of the park was bought by the Croydon Corporation as a dumping place for their sewage, and the inner portion and advowson by Sir Henry Bridges, who fenced it and let it for dairy farming. The canal-like lake in front of the house was drained. The southern arable lands, which had once been the common fields of the Manor, now enclosed as New Barn Farm were purchased by the Collyer-Bristow family who owned a mansion and small estate on the corner of Plough Lane. The pictures, which included two attributed to Holbein, and a number of other portraits, were sold off, together with the furnishings. The oak panelling was stripped from the walls of the great hall and bought by a village builder, one Mr. Juggins. During the period that it stood empty, a claimant to the estate named John Chalkwright, with the connivance of the verger and his wife, forced an entry and squatted for a while in a state of high revelry. A prospectus was issued on his behalf by a Croydon lawyer, George Dixon, offering a life annuity in the estates whose rentals were said to exceed £200,000 each year. Despite the attractive terms there were few takers and Chalkwright's masquerade came to an end when the Steward, Mr. Glasscock, aided by a posse of labourers, forcibly ejected him from the mansion. Or was it a masquerade? From the time of Mrs. Gee onwards there was no blood relationship to the earlier family, and it would be surprising if there were not others with a better claim. There was, for instance, a George Carew whose daughters Sarah and Rebecca were christened in St. Mary's Church in 1789 and 1791. A George Carew, almost certainly the same, appears as owner of an estate in Keston in 1798 which in 1780 had belonged to Richard Gee Carew and reverted to him in 1810. John Chalkwright was described as a labourer and the 'proofs documentary and otherwise' offered on his behalf are no longer available. A son born to Isabella, his daughter, was registered as Sir Richard Carew Percival and he has living descendants who still claim that they are the last true survivors of the Beddington Carews.

The house and twenty acres of land were finally bought by the Royal Female Orphanage for the sum of £14,500 but while work was in progress on the restoration of the ruinous north wing, a fire broke out at the opposite end of the mansion. The local paper reported on 17th May 1865 that about half-past four in the morning the end rooms of the south wing were discovered to be on fire. "At 10 o'clock when we visited the spot the fire brigade was just taking its departure ... The flames had not been allowed to spread far, but where they had reached, the demolition of the timbers and woodwork of the house was complete, the immense beams were several of them lying about reduced to crumbling masses of charcoal, and the walls and the rafters were reeking with steam from the saturation from the engine."

It was now necessary to rebuild almost the whole of the mansion except for the Tudor Hall which had again escaped. In the rebuild the baroque appearance was totally destroyed and the mansion took on its heavy Victorian version of domestic Tudor. The wrought-iron gates that once linked both wings were removed and sold to America, the Carew achievement that surmounted them being passed to the Devonshire branch of the family. In their place, the present linking corridor was built. The remodelled house was formally opened as an orphanage by the Duke of Cambridge in June 1866.

Charlie Carew retained the Manor of Walton for ten years after the sale, then it too was auctioned off. The wretched holder of the name lingered on for another two years, dying in a London lodging house in April 1872. His body was brought to Beddington for burial amongst his ancestors, real and adopted. It was a cold day, with flurries of snow, and old Baldwin, an estate worker, was called across by the undertaker's men to assist them in re-arranging the contents of the vault to make room for the latest arrival. The wooden trap-door in the Carew chapel was prised open and the three men descended into the vault to stack up the coffins of the long-dead members of the family. It was unpleasant work, for the chamber was partially waterlogged, and it had to be done quickly in order to be ready for the funeral cortège. Not unthankfully, perhaps, the Rev. Canon A. H. Bridges, rector and wealthiest man in the village, ordered, soon after the ceremony, that the vault be sealed off by pouring liquid concrete into the cavities.

So was buried Charles Hallowell Hallowell Carew at the age of 41. All the devices of adoption, change of name, and entailment of the estates, could not keep the Carews in Beddington. There is a sadness about endings, whether it be of individuals or of institutions, but by the mid-nineteenth century the family had ceased to be relevant to the life around them. The district's first steam railway between Croydon and Epsom began to puff along the tracks in 1847, bisecting the Carew land and bringing changes to the Hamlet of Wallington where the inclosure of the open fields (in 1853) swept away the last traces of medieval agriculture. White villas proliferated around the rose-covered station, heralding the beginnings of urban development, and in 1867 Wallington was instituted as

OPENING OF THE FEMALE ORPHAN ASYLUM, BEDDINGTON, BY THE DUKE OF CAMBRIDGE.

36. *The rebuilt house, opened in 1866 as the Female Orphan Asylum*

a separate parish. Between 1851 and 1871 the population doubled, to double again during the next decade. Change was slower around Beddington, where the Collyer-Bristows, the Bridges, the Meeks and Trittons, with their large houses and gardens kept the urban tide at bay. Agriculture remained important, particularly in the southern parts of the parish, though the cultivation of lavender, camomile and mint replaced corn as principal crops.

To the men who toiled in the fields and gathered nightly in the old Plough Inn some things did not change. Each year William Pile, local newsagent, wrote a summary of the year's events as a preface to his Directory and in 1885 he noted: "the fine summer weather and still finer autumn has given the field worker plenty to do and there has been less distress amongst the working classes than sometimes." Later he wrote: "The long severe frost in January and February has put the poor to test." Five centuries earlier the village reeve probably used similar terms in his report to Nicholas Carreu, and five hundred years before that, the Bishop wrote "now of the cattle that has survived this severe winter . . .". To the victims of the season, the loves, obligations, troubles, finances and serio-comic military endeavours of their gentry no doubt provided enjoyable topics for gossip, but what really mattered was survival.

The Rev. H. Dodd has contributed so much to this work in spirit, that it is right that the final words should come from him. "The dust of armed horsemen, the merry jest of kings, the hushed whispers of ambassadors, the tattle and gossip of pedlars as they hawked their wares, have all passed this way; and Beddington folk have stared at them in wonder, passed their comments and made an honest profit out of them; all sleep together in the dust. And we are heirs of all of them."

Appendix I: Who were the parents of Nicholas Carreu?

None of the suggested parents of the founder of the Beddington line is entirely satisfactory and I am grateful to Mrs. J. A. Carew Richardson for calling my attention to this fact, and for supplying much other genealogical information.

The certain facts are that Nicholas was a younger son, that he is first mentioned in association with the Beddington Portionist in 1349, that he died in 1390 and that he had a brother named John who predeceased him and who was buried at Beddington. He can hardly have been born much earlier than 1310, nor later than 1331. Vivian's 'Devon and Cornwall Pedigrees' are based on manuscripts collected during the seventeenth century by George Carew, Earl of Totnes. These named the Sir Nicholas Carew who died in 1311 as the father of our Nicholas and most later writers agree with this statement. But the Beddington Carews quartered the arms of Mohun on their escutcheon and, unless there was collusion with the Heralds, a thing not unknown, the Mohun connection does not occur until the next generation. Further, the Sir John who was the elder brother of this Nicholas died in 1323 long before there was any association between Beddington and the Carews.

This Sir John had two recorded sons, a Nicholas who died young, and another Sir John who is given by Lysons as the founder of the Beddington dynasty. Sir John was a minor when he claimed his father's estates in 1327 (see D.N.B.) and died in 1363. His eldest son John died in France (or perhaps Ireland) c.1346 and there seems no reason why his body should have been brought to Beddington for burial. It is possible that there was a fourth unrecorded son born after the death of John the Soldier, probably by Sir John's second wife, and therefore half brother to our Nicholas. The list of Portionists in Beddington (Manning and Bray) shows 'John de Carru' as the next-named holder of the office after William de Carru, and gives 1375 as the date of his death. This must surely be the John, buried in St. Mary's Church near whom Nicholas wished to lie. As a youngest son who entered the church and died without progeny, it is not unreasonable to find that he is omitted from the pedigrees.

The dates fit, but only just. Sir John must have produced his three sons in rapid succession before he became legally of age (in 1333). A later date for the birth of Nicholas cannot be reconciled with his employment in legal business with William in 1349, and this is the weak link in the chain. Vivian gives the date of birth of Sir Leonard as 1343. If true, one must accept with its contradictions, his statement that Sir Nicholas who died 1311 was the father, and also that John Carru, priest, was not the brother John near whom Nicholas asked to be buried.

There is a third possibility, however, which will make generations of Carews turn in their vaults. This is that the Beddington Nicholas and John were in fact the sons of William the Priest. William's interest in Nicholas was great; he is associated with him in land transactions exactly in the way that Nicholas was later to act with his own son. During his wilder youth, William had time to marry and bury a wife before being ordained, but it may not have been politic for one who was obviously hoping for high office to advertise openly his progeny, and later generations of the family may have felt a similar embarrassment—hence the ambiguity.

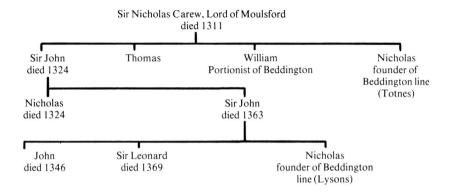

Sir Nicholas Carew, Lord of Moulsford
died 1311

Sir John
died 1324

Thomas

William
Portionist of Beddington

Nicholas
founder of
Beddington line
(Totnes)

Nicholas
died 1324

Sir John
died 1363

John
died 1346

Sir Leonard
died 1369

Nicholas
founder of Beddington
line (Lysons)

Appendix II: Coats of arms of the Carew family

The Carew arms are, in heraldic terms, or, three lioncells passant in pale sable, and for the less well instructed, three black lions on a golden shield; their motto 'Non Conscrire Sibi' meant 'to be conscious of no guilt'. It was common for the husband to impale his arms with those of his wife, that is, to show both arms upon a half-shield each, and for the son to quarter both coats. Strictly the quartering should imply inheritance of lands through an heiress, but arms were often bequeathed and, despite visitation by the heralds sometimes wrongly assumed. As a family of ancient and baronial origin they had the right to use two red antelopes as supporters on either side of their shield (a right normally reserved for peers). Above the shield is a knight's helmet mantled in red and silver and above this the curious crest of the topmast head of a ship from which issues a demi-lion rampant flanked on either side by three half pikes.

Earlier members of the family must have quartered Huscarle (azure, three battle axes argent) but this had been dropped by the time of Sir Francis Carew, though the family of St. John continued to display both Carew and Huscarle upon their escutcheon, as may be seen in the memorial window to Viscount Bolingbroke in Battersea Parish Church. Lord Bolingbroke's ancestors included Sanctia Carew who was the wife of John Iwardby whose daughter Jane married Sir John St. John. The Huscarle shield was probably crowded out by the more distinguished arms at the time of Sir Richard Carew who had the right to number Lord Hoo and Lord Welles amongst his forbears. Sir Francis also added the arms of his mother Elizabeth Bryan. His tomb also has the effigies of Sir Nicholas Throckmorton Carew and family, above whose heads is a shield quartering Throckmorton, Carew, More, and Oxenbridge (their father, grandmother, mother, and great-grandmother respectively).

The last Carews seem to have adopted the shield of Sir Francis with small variations. Sir Nicholas Carew Bt. (d.1727) placed the shield of his wife in pretence upon his arms, as may be seen in the Great Hall, while his son dropped Malmaynes in order to add Oxenbridge and Hacket as is displayed on his memorial tablet.

115

The escutcheon of Sir Francis (d.1611) is as follows:
1. Carew 2. Idrone (spelt Hidron by some commentators) 3. Mohun (H. W. Pointer in S.A. C.61 queries the right of the Beddington Carews to the arms of Mohun, probably because he accepts the Manning and Bray genealogy) 4. Hoo 5. St. Maur or St. Omer 6. Malmaynes 7. Wichingham 8. St. Leger (These probably came through the now extinct barony of Hoo) 9. Welles 10. Engayne 11. Waterton (probably from Lord Welles) 12. Bryan.

37. The achievement of Sir Nicholas Carew 1st Baronet 1687-1727

38. *The Carews' house Royal Female Orphanage in the early 20th century. It is used today as Carew Manor Special School*

Appendix III: Genealogy of the Carews

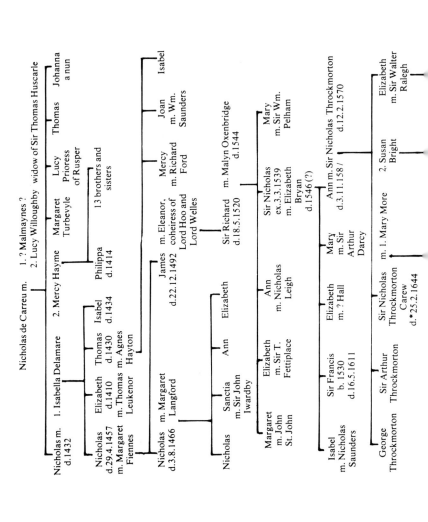

Family tree / genealogical chart

Thomas

Elizabeth
Carew
Ralegh

Mary d.1631

Elizabeth

Oliphe d.1670

Edmund d.1654

George

Lionel   Elizabeth   4 others

Nicholas d.1643

Francis

Sir Francis
d.* 9.4.1649
m. Susan
Romney
d.23.12.1687

Frances d.1641

Philippa d.1655

Elizabeth d.1641

Susan

Rebecca
m. Thomas
Temple

Sir Nicholas
b.30.6.1635
d.9.1.1687
m. Susan Isham

Richard d.1689

Nicholas
m. Anne
Lennard
both d.
1721

Philippa
m. Richard
Gee

Jane d.1689

Justiniana d.1668

Susan d.1659

Sir Francis
b.12.9.1663
d.29.9.1689
m. Ann Boteler
d.1689

Richard Gee
m.? Holt

Boteler d.1689

Elizabeth
b.4.5.1688
m. John
Fountain

an infant
d.12.12.1689

Sir Nicholas
b.6.2.1687
d.18.3.1727
m. Elizabeth
Hacket
d.10.2.1740

Ann m.1. Thomas Fountain 2. Joshua Ward

Nicholas
d.1715

Elizabeth
d.1712

Sir Nicholas
b.1720
d.8.8.1762
m. Catherine
Martin
d.18.3.1762

John
Fountain
m. Ann
Montague

Frances
Fountain

Thomas
Fountain d.1780

Richard Gee
Carew
d.1816

William Gee
m. Anne Paston Gould
d.28.3.1828
bequeathed the estates
to her cousin

Elizabeth
b.8.3.1745
d.* 6.12.1752

Catherine
b.20.5.1742
d.3.3.1769

Sir Benjamin Hallowell
(Carew)
d.2.9.1834
m.? Inglefield

Charles Hallowell Carew
b.1802   d.1849

Charles Hallowell Hallowell Carew
b.1831   d.April 1872

b   date of baptism
d   date of death
d* date of burial

Bibliography

The standard works that have formed the basis of this account are as follows:

A History of the County of Surrey by John Aubrey, first published 1718 (Aubrey)

A Tour through the Whole Island of Britain by Daniel Defoe. 1723 (Defoe)

The Environs of London by Rev. Daniel Lysons. 1796 (Lysons)

The History of Surrey by Rev. Owen Manning and William Bray 1804-14 (Manning & Bray)

The Victoria History of the County of Surrey ed. H. E. Malden 1902-1912 (VCH)

The Dictionary of National Biography (DNB)

The Surrey Archaeological Collections (SAC) are published by the Surrey Archaeological Society. The principal articles only are quoted.

A History of Beddington by Rev. T. Bentham. 1923 (Bentham)

Historical Notes on Wallington by Rev. John Williams. 1873 (Williams)

Chapter 1

The version of Carew origins given here comes from the Biographica Britannica of 1784 and derives from the Chronicle by Giraldus Cambriensis. The Dictionary of National Biography gives an alternative account which makes Gerald marry the sister of Nest; most genealogies of this period are very dubious. The letter by Bishop Denewulf is printed in English Historical Documents Vol. I. edited by Dorothy Whitelock. The complete manorial descent of Beddington manors is given in the Victoria County History. The careers of William de Carreu and Nicholas in this and the following chapter have been reconstructed from the calendars of close and patent rolls. The background to this account derives from Life on the English Manor by H. S. Bennett, The Black Death by Philip Ziegler and The Age of Chivalry by Sir Arthur Bryant. The Beddington Portion by Keith Pryer, published by the Beddington, Carshalton and Wallington Archaeological Society examines the sources of this longstanding bone of contention between the Rector and his patrons.

Chapter 2

The Taxation Returns for 1332 are published by the Surrey Record Society while Keith Muckelroy wrote an article Woodcote, a Lost Village published by the Bourne Society in their Local Records. Keith Pryer (op cit.) discusses the layout of medieval Beddington. The Berkshire Victoria History gives some details of the Huscarles and Carews, and the Record Office of that county has some Carew correspondence and a rent roll of Simon Roce. The will of Nicolas Carreu appears in the Dodd Papers, a copy of which is held by the Sutton Central Library. Some details of the politics of the time appear in an article Wycliffe and the Lollards by Peter Heidtmann in History Today October 1970. England in the Age of Chaucer by William Woods gives a wealth of detail, while many readers will enjoy Anya Seton's beautifully researched novel Katherine.

Chapter 3

Croydon Homes of the Past by Clarence C. Paget is the source throughout for the Manor of Norbury; his work is also most fully documented for the early Carews. The

Memorial Brasses of Surrey by Mill Stephenson was published in the Surrey Archaeological Collections. SAC 25 deals with Beddington with a further correction in SAC 33. James Carew is best dealt with in the Sussex Archaeological Collections Vol. VIII. See also Richard III by Paul Murray Kendal for details of the Wars of the Roses.

Chapter 4

The career of Sir Nicholas is outlined in all the histories of Surrey already mentioned and he receives full treatment in the Biographica Britannica (op cit.) The best account, fully documented, is in the Dictionary of National Biography which has also an account of Sir Peter Carew and other West Country relatives. The contemporary Chronicle by Edward Hall was published by the Camden Society in 1875. The books dealing with Henry VIII are legion but not all give Carew any prominence, and some writers, who should know better, confuse him with his Cornish cousins. Some which have useful details are Henry VIII by Francis Hacket, Fanfare for Elizabeth by Edith Sitwell, Henry VIII and his Court by Neville Williams, and A History of Greenwich by Beryl Platt. The Collections of Ordinances and Regulations for the Government of the Royal Households (Society of Antiquaries (1790), gives an account of the duties expected of his various offices. His trial, with the comments by Chapuys is contained in the Dodd Papers. The collection of Carew papers from the 15th to the 19th centuries made by Sir Thomas Phillipps was sold and dispersed after his death. Many are now in the Surrey Record Office, and some are in Sutton Central Library.

Chapter 5

Carew's speech from the scaffold comes from a Document in the Library of Corpus Christi College, Cambridge, and is reproduced by permission of the Master and Fellows of that College. It is part of a letter from Sir Robert Chester to Archbishop Parker (Parker MS CCCC MS 100). William Shakespeare gives some useful tips on the psychology of Tudor crowds on similar occasions. The letters to Cromwell are from the Dodd Papers. Bentham gives a few extra details while Mary's order for the return of the estates is from Patent Rolls 871.

Chapter 6

Thomas Mabson's Accounts and the Inventory of the Hall are printed by Bentham from documents then in his possession. The Carew Household book was the subject of an article by Sir Henry Lambert in SAC Vol. 31. The Dictionary of National Biography has an entry on Sir Nicholas Throckmorton. Ralegh and the Throckmortons by A. L. Rowse has been an invaluable source of details on both those names, and of Nicholas Throckmorton Carew and his sister. The England of Elizabeth by the same author provides much background as does Elizabethan Life in Town and Country by M. St. Clare Byrne and Elizabeth Burton's The Elizabethans at Home. The account of the Armada emergency in Surrey draws upon Manning and Bray and on the Loseley Papers and Laing Manuscripts that were carefully preserved by Sir William More.

Chapter 7

Books on Ralegh are as numerous as those on Henry VIII. That by Rowse has already been cited. Sir Walter Ralegh by Robert Lacey and a book of the same title by

Norman Lloyd Douglas have been most useful. Brief Lives by John Aubrey must also be mentioned. The anecdote of Elizabeth and the cherries has been retailed many times and seems to occur first in an article by John Gibson in Archaelogia Volume XII who visited at the end of the seventeenth century. The meeting between James and Ralegh I was inclined to disbelieve although it is given by Bentham; however Rowse also refers to it and it may therefore be accepted. Nicholas' despairing letter to his father-in-law was preserved by him in the Loseley Papers. The attempt on the Wandle waters was written up by M. S. Guiseppi in SAC Vol. 21.

Chapter 8

The will of Sir Francis appears in SAC Vol. 35 with additional details in Manning and Bray. Bentham also gives details of some of the legacies from documents then in his possession which are supplemented by the Phillipps Papers in Surrey Record Office. The Laing Manuscripts II 637/4 and the Berkshire Record Office are the source of the anecdotes of Sir Nicholas and his village. The letter from Lady Ralegh is quoted by Manning and Bray while the biographies of Ralegh already quoted give details of his execution. Miss Wotton wrote a letter to The Times of October 1918 explaining the case for Ralegh's burial at Beddington. It is reprinted as an appendix by Bentham. The macabre account of the head is from Manning and Bray.

Chapter 9

Details of Sir Nicholas's Croydon neighbours are from Paget (op cit.), while an article by Bernard Nurse in The London Recusant Vol. III No. 3 and the unpublished Surrey during the Civil War by my son A. R. Michell refer to other areas. Manuscript sources in this chapter are many. They include The Carshalton Parish registers, Sequestration Papers 28245 and the Journal of the House of Commons. The Will of Sir Nicholas is a British Museum Additional Manuscript 29605. Warwick's List of repairs to the Manor House is a recent purchase by Surrey Record Office while an account of his life appears in the Dictionary of National Biography. The Beddington Vestry Book is held in Sutton Central Library.

Chapter 10

The British Museum holds the Account Book of Sir Nicholas Carew which was written up in SAC Vol. 10. The museum also holds the Carew Correspondence transcribed by Dodd. Dr. Leng has an entry in the Dictionary of National Biography, while the account of Beddington in 1723 was provided by his curate for Bishop Willis' Visitation, SAC Vol. 39. Background for this chapter is from Hogarth's England by D. Jarrat, the monumental Johnson's England ed. by A. S. Turbeville and London Life in the Eighteenth Century by M. D. George.

Chapter 11

The description of Carew Manor in the early nineteenth century is from Unwin's Guide to the Beauties of Britain (1813) and from Lysons, both are quoted by E. Walford in his Greater London Vol. II. The troubles of Nicholas Hacket Carew are from Dodd and from SAC Vol. 28 and an article by Lord Onslow in SAC Vol. 40. The Will of Carew was communicated by Mrs. Richardson. The tithe dispute is referred to by Manning and

Bray and examined by Keith Pryer (op cit.).

Chapter 12

Bentham gives personal details of the later Carews. For development of the district see The Book of the Wandle by J. M. Hobson, The Wandle Guide published by Sutton Library and Arts Services, and my own Beddington in 1837 published by the Beddington, Carshalton and Wallington Archaeological Society. Historical notes on Wallington by J. Williams is also quoted. Sutton Central Library have photostats of the Tithe Map 1840, the Deed for the Inclosure of Beddington and the Catalogue of the Carew Sale. Sir Benjamin Hallowell Carew has an entry in the Dictionary of National Biography. For background to the later chapters see The Parish Chest by W. E. Tate and Surrey in 1815 by A. H. Lock.

INDEX

(Illustrations are indicated by page numbers in **bold** type)

INDEX

126

INDEX